DATE DUE

60 on Up

Also by Lillian B. Rubin, Ph.D.

The Man with the Beautiful Voice: And More Stories from the Other Side of the Couch

Tangled Lives: Daughters, Mothers, and the Crucible of Aging

The Transcendent Child: Tales of Triumph Over the Past

Families on the Fault Line: America's Working Class Speaks about the Family, the Economy, Race, and Ethnicity

Erotic Wars: What Happened to the Sexual Revolution?

Quiet Rage: Bernie Goetz in a Time of Madness

Just Friends: The Role of Friendship in Our Lives

Intimate Strangers: Men and Women Together

Women of a Certain Age: The Midlife Search for Self

Worlds of Pain: Life in the Working-Class Family

Busing & Backlash: White against White in an Urban School District

60 on Up

The Truth about Aging in America

Lillian B. Rubin, Ph.D.

Beacon Press
Boston

Beacon Press
25 Beacon Street
Boston, Massachusetts 02108-2892
www.beacon.org

Beacon Press books
are published under the auspices of
the Unitarian Universalist Association of Congregations.

10 09 08 07   8 7 6 5 4 3 2 1

This book is printed on acid-free paper that meets the uncoated paper
ANSI/NISO specifications for permanence as revised in 1992.

Text design by Tag Savage
Composition by Wilsted & Taylor Publishing Services

Library of Congress Cataloging-in-Publication Data
Rubin, Lillian B.
  60 on up : the truth about aging in America / Lillian Rubin.
    p. cm.
  Includes bibliographical references.
  ISBN-13: 978-0-8070-2928-2
    1. Older people—Psychology. 2. Older people—Conduct of life.
  3. Older people—Attitudes. 4. Aging. I. Title.
HQ1061.R83 2007
305.26—dc22   2007013570

An earlier article featuring some of the themes in chapter 6
appeared in *Dissent* (fall 2006), 88–94.

For Marci and Hank

*And for all those everywhere
who are struggling with this new stage of life.*

Contents

Chapter One

Through the
Looking Glass

G etting old sucks! It always has, it always will. Yes, I know
about all those books and articles extolling the wonders of
what the media call the "new old age." I've been reading them for
quite a while now and can only conclude that they're either written by forty-year-olds who, like children afraid of the dark, draw
rosy pictures as they try to convince themselves that no unknown
monsters await them. Or they're lying. Is that too harsh a word?
Perhaps. Maybe it's not a lie but a wish, a hope, a need to believe
there's something more to this business of getting old than we see
around us.

I recall Betty Friedan's visit to San Francisco shortly after the
publication of *The Fountain of Age*,[1] a book proclaiming old age
as a vital time of life at the same time that she herself was unable
to walk the two blocks from her hotel to the restaurant where
we were to have lunch. As I helped her to her chair, I said,
with all the irony at my command, "*The Fountain of Age*, huh?"
She shrugged, "What would you want me to write, that it sucks?
There's got to be more than that."

Not that I don't believe in the possibility of what Friedan called a "vital old age." It just seems to me to be half the story. Nor do I quarrel with her argument that for too long we've looked at old age solely through the lens of decline. But it's also true that old age—even now when old age isn't quite what it used to be —*is* a time of decline and loss. To deny that, to look away from the reality in favor of some new one-dimensional view of aging, serves us ill.

Getting old probably isn't something anyone in any society looks forward to, but for us Americans, it seems downright un-American. I was reminded anew how the distaste for aging and the old colors our national thinking, whether about social policy or television programming, when I opened my copy of the *New York Times* one morning, turned to the Op-Ed page, as I always do, and saw yet another reminder of what a trial we old folks are. There at the top of the page was a sketch of an old man dozing in his recliner and an attention-getting sidebar: "Geezers: Don't even think of getting near that remote." Just below it, in an article titled "My Plan to Save Network Television," the author, a television writer and producer, takes a satirical look at advertisers' and TV executives' pursuit of the "key demographic," people eighteen to forty-nine. He writes:

> People over 49 do not buy interesting products. They detract from the hip environment advertisers seek. . . . The fact is, mature viewers are threatening the well-being of network television. I have a bold but common-sense suggestion: old people should not be allowed to watch TV. I anticipate the predictable charges of "discriminatory," "unfair," "idiotic." Well, millions of elderly people live in age-restricted retirement communities, and you don't hear young people whining about that. Right-thinking older Americans will see this as a chance to do something for their country.

Nurturing a nation's consumer base is as vital as protecting its streams and forests. It's time for people over 49 "to take one for the team."[2]

Tongue in cheek? Certainly. Funny? Sure. Did I smile when I read it? Yes, with tears in my eyes and anger in my heart because, like all good humor, it rests on a profound truth.

So even though we old folks have plenty of money to spend— $2 trillion a year, according to the *Times* article—we can't even get a network executive to care what we think because we don't spend it in the right places. Hmmm. Where are all those sources of personal power and self-esteem I keep hearing about as the media celebrate the glories of the "new old age"?

Our revulsion with aging, our flight from it at almost any cost, is deeply ingrained. Yes, I know "revulsion" is a strong word. But think about it: who *wants* to be old? What do you think when you look in the mirror and see the signs of your own aging? How does it make you feel? Do you want to turn away, rush off to the nearest cosmetics counter and buy up every cream that promises to remove the lines that are so distressing, run to the gym in the hope that you can stave off the sagging muscles, call the plastic surgeon your friend used? Do you say to yourself, as a fifty-year-old woman said to me when explaining why she's planning plastic surgery, "I try not to look at myself when I put my lipstick on, but sometimes I can't help it. Then I think: *That can't be me.* It's disorienting. I don't recognize that person in the mirror as me; she's not me, or at least not the image I have of me. And I want that one back. I want the outside to match the inside."

I want the outside to match the inside. What is that about? Why, when we've lived through so many years, overcome so many trials, does our internal image register only our younger selves? Why do we want it to? Why not some composite picture that takes in all the changes we've gone through along the way? Why are we so appalled at the signs of aging that we're willing to undergo painful and expensive surgical procedures? Why, when people are in their last throes, are they still saying, as a friend who was close to death remarked to me a few years ago, "How can I be dying when inside I still feel like I did when I was twenty?"

In her groundbreaking book, *The Coming of Age*, written in the early 1970s, Simone de Beauvoir speaks passionately about the loss of our identity in old age, our fear of it, our inability (unwillingness?) to believe that the self we knew is gone, replaced by a loathsome stranger we can't recognize, who can't possibly be the person we've known until now. Writes de Beauvoir:

> Thinking of myself as an old person . . . means thinking of myself as someone else, as *an other* than myself. Every metamorphosis has something frightening about it. . . . But when one is young the real advantages of the adult status usually counterbalance the wish to remain oneself, unchanged. Whereas old age looms ahead like a calamity: even among those who are thought well preserved, age brings with it a very obvious physical decline. . . . When we look at the image of our own future provided by the old we do not believe it: an absurd inner voice whispers that *that* will never happen to us—when *that* happens it will no longer be ourselves that it happens to.[3]

Why is it so agonizingly difficult to accept? Is it simply natural to prefer youth and beauty to old age and decline? A look across cultures suggests there may be some truth in that, but if so, it doesn't explain the intensity of the aversion with which we look upon old age. Perhaps, then, it's something more complicated, something more psychological that's related to our anxiety about our mortality. Accepting our own aging may come too close to the realization that life is finite and that we'll soon reach its limit—a truth that's extremely difficult for most Americans, perhaps most people in Western society, to bear.

But psychology doesn't stand alone, isn't given life outside of a cultural context. A core maxim of social psychology is that what we think about a person influences how we see him, how we see him affects how we behave toward him, and how we behave toward him ultimately shapes how he feels about himself, if not actually who he is. It's in this interaction between self and society that we can see most clearly how social attitudes toward the old give form and definition to how we feel about ourselves. For what we see in the faces of others will eventually mark our own.

As a sociologist, I have been a student of aging for almost four decades; as a psychologist during much of this same period, I saw more than a few patients who were struggling with the issues aging brings; as a writer, I've written about many subjects, including a memoir about old age,[4] and for the last decade or so I've been living in the territory and have talked to dozens of people about their experience of aging. Yet I didn't fully realize how much ageism had become the signature mark of oppression in our society until I began to interview people more systematically and listened to the stories they had to tell,[5] stories that forced me back on myself and my own prejudice about old people, even though I am also one of them.

I am one of them. Even now, after all I've learned, the words on the page bring a small shock and something inside resists. I want to take the words back, to say, "No, it's not true, I'm really not like *them*," and explain all the ways I'm different from the old woman you saw struggling up the stairs on the subway or bus this morning, the one you looked away from with a slight sense of distaste.

Old age has probably never been a comfortable place in a society that glorifies youth, but until recently we didn't live there very long. At the dawn of the twentieth century, the median age at death was just over forty-nine years; now it's close to eighty and rising rapidly. Then, 13 percent of people who reached sixty-five would live to see eighty-five. Now, nearly half of the sixty-five-year-olds can expect to live that long.[6] Measured in evolutionary time, this near-doubling of the life span is nothing less than a demographic miracle—an astonishing, exhilarating, frightening miracle.

While the sixty-five-year-olds are coming onstage, those over eighty-five presently represent the fastest growing segment of our population, having increased their numbers by nearly 40 percent in the single decade between 1990 and 2000.[7] Even one hundred is no longer a wistful dream, for while the actual proportion of centenarians is still small, their numbers, too, are rising fast enough to suggest another miracle in the making.[8]

This book tells the story of aging in America in the twenty-first century. It's about a new stage of life, one whose path few have ever walked before. It's about the struggle to cut through the thicket of the social and psychological impediments along the way. It's about the search to find meaning and purpose as the years march on, about the deeply embedded cultural norms and expectations that hamper that search. And it's about the costs of the new longevity to those who are now old, to their children coming up behind them so quickly, to their grandchildren who are at the bottom layer of the sandwich that makes up these generations, and not least to the society that will soon be forced to make room for them.

Chapter Two

Out of the Closet

I sometimes think the story of aging in our time is a tale of "yes, buts..." Yes, the fact that we live longer, healthier lives is something to celebrate, but it's not without its costs, both public and private. Yes, the definition of "old" has been pushed back, but no matter where we place it, our social attitudes and our private angst about getting old largely remain intact.

If a public conversation on aging is to have any value, we need to talk about how much has changed and how little, about the social and psychological meanings of living so long and how they interact with each other in a society that, at best, is ambivalent about its old. We need to think aloud about the impact of our increasingly long life span on those who follow us, about the pleasures, the pains, and the many sorrows this stage of life brings, about the gift our expanded life span has bestowed upon us and the significant costs that accompany it.

But instead of complexity, we get oversimple tales about the wonders of the "new old age," along with treatises on "age power" and tips on how to make these "the power years."[1] I sometimes think old age is two different countries. There's the real old age for those of us who live there and know its conflicts and contradictions. Then there's the old age of those who write about it, most of them middle-aged women and men who live a long way from my country and are so frightened of coming to it that they grasp at half truths and offer them up as if they were the whole story.

Until recently, aging and old age lived largely in the social closet. But with 78 million baby boomers—that huge cohort that shaped everything it touched as it swept through society, the one that thought it would be forever young when it coined the mantra "You can't trust anyone over thirty"—now turning sixty, silence is no longer possible.

As this best educated, most literate, and largest generation in history moves toward old age, concerns about our long life span have come center stage. Economists worry about the impact of our increasingly aging population on the nation's productivity; politicians wring their public hands about how the old will soon bankrupt what's left of our social welfare system; and some of the younger generations, many of whom don't believe they'll ever be old, complain that there will be nothing left for them. Occasionally, too, we read about the abuse of the old—a nursing home where residents are seriously mistreated, a famous family in which a 53-year-old man accuses his 82-year-old father of abusing his 104-year-old mother[2]—and we're appropriately horrified.

But while the wealthy and prominent make headlines, the 1 to 3 million older Americans who are abused by their caregivers go largely unnoticed.[3] For like the homeless, those who are already old are mostly not in our social sights, except maybe when they do something to call attention to themselves, like make demands on the public treasury for such things as insurance to cover prescription drugs. We have an epithet for them then: "greedy geezers," coined a decade or so ago by then-senator Alan K. Simpson. Or when they walk irritatingly slowly as they board the bus or the subway. We're impatient, wishing they'd get out of our busy way, out of sight, and we look away, repelled, loath to see what could be our future.

In his highly regarded treatise, *Aging and Old Age*, Richard Posner considers "the factors that from a rational-choice perspective are likely to influence the treatment the elderly will receive from society." It makes "biological sense," he writes, that while we're "genetically programmed" to protect the young, we're not similarly wired toward protection of the old. "Inclusive fitness is unlikely to be promoted by the devotion of huge resources to the survival of persons who, by reason of advanced age, are not reproductively or otherwise productive, either actually or (like children) potentially."[4]

Strip away the awkward language and what you have is a cold calculus that we're not worth the cost, whatever that may be. Small wonder we so fiercely resist the idea of being old. Who wants to be invisible? Or to have so little social value? Or to be criticized as greedy when all you've asked for is something citizens of every other Western democracy take for granted?

Both Friedan and Posner published their work on aging in the early 1990s when it was already clear that we were witnessing a demographic revolution in the making. By 2007 it had arrived. Over 36 million Americans—12 percent of the total population —presently are over sixty-five. In the single year between 2003 and 2004, 351,000 people arrived at the cusp of old age. This before the first of the baby boomers begin to reach that milestone. After that the numbers skyrocket. The Census Bureau projects that by 2050, 86.7 million people, roughly 21 percent of the projected population at that time, will be sixty-five or older. That's an increase of 147 percent over the present number. Compare that to the population as a whole, which will have increased by only 49 percent over the same period.[5]

Given the drama of these demographics and their implication

for the future of our society and the people who live in it, it's no surprise that age is on our collective mind big time these days. Predictions vary depending on the mind-set of the predictors, on whether they see the glass as half full or half empty. The pessimists see disaster as they warn of the crises that lie in wait: The financial burdens on the social system will prove unsupportable. Medicare and Social Security will go broke. The economy will falter as the nonproductive old outnumber the productive young. The burden on families will be intolerable as sixty-five-year-olds find themselves the caregivers for their eighty-five-year-old parents at the same time that they're worrying about their future and how they'll support their own old age.

Those who see a half-full glass tell us the worries are overblown. Sure, they say, the social institutions designed to ease the old age of earlier generations, whether health care, housing, or social security, are not adequate to deal with the huge aging population that looms ahead. But with the political will and sensible planning, old programs can morph into new ones that will meet the realities of our continually expanding life span.

True, the optimists grant, many sixty-five-year-olds are caring for eighty-year-old parents, but 60 percent of those over eighty continue to live independently. They agree, too, that the ratio of those over sixty-five to what we now call "the working-age population" will nearly double in the next fifty years. But, the optimists remind the pessimists, the working-age population is already being redefined upward, as witness the legislation outlawing age discrimination, the disappearance of mandatory age-based retirement in government and industry, and the increase in the age at which Americans can claim Social Security benefits. With the promise of an aging population that is heartier, healthier, and better educated than ever before, it's reasonable to assume, the optimists insist, that increasing numbers will remain in the work force.

Maybe, maybe not, the pessimists reply. Ask the 40 percent of sixty-five-year-olds who are taking care of their aged parents and you'll hear another tune. In fact, even those whose parents live independently find themselves preoccupied with their welfare, worrying about a future they know is coming, wondering how they'll manage when it does. What's more, the idea of being on the job until eighty and beyond may appeal to a Supreme Court justice or a world-famous television journalist, but is that what the average person, whose job is neither so important nor so glamorous, wants to do with these newfound years?

The arguments continue, but they're more form than content. No matter which side of the optimist/pessimist divide they fall on, everyone agrees that something new is emerging, something we might call the next life stage, the one that never existed before, the one for which we have no name and no template. We're living longer but doing it better, getting older but staying younger, and no one quite knows what to do about it—not even whether it's a blessing or a curse.

While the experts talk, those of us who are old are busy living the reality of aging in a society that worships youth and pitches it, packages it, and sells it so relentlessly that the anti-aging industry is the hottest growth ticket in town. Think that's hyperbole? Plug the term "anti-aging" into Google and you'll come up with over 3 million hits.

From the scientists tucked away in their labs who, with the aid of federal dollars, search for the key to yet a longer life, to the seventeen thousand physicians and scientists who are members of the recently spawned American Academy of Anti-Aging Medicine, whose Web site boasts that "aging is not inevitable" but "a treatable medical disease,"[6] to the plastic surgeons who exist to serve our illusion that if we don't *look* old, we won't *be* or *feel* old, to the multibillion-dollar cosmetics industry whose creams and potions promise to wipe out our wrinkles and massage away our cellulite, to the fashion designers who have turned yesterday's size ten into today's size six so that forty-year-old women can delude themselves into believing they still wear the same size they wore in college,[7] to the media pundits who have recently taken to assuring us that sixty really isn't sixty anymore—the old and those who soon will be counted among them are big business, at least insofar as anti-aging products and services are concerned.

And if that isn't enough, the *New York Times* features a front-page article about the latest boon to the American entrepreneurial spirit:[3] a growing array of "brain health" programs on Internet sites, in "brain gyms," workshops, and fitness camps, an increasingly robust business in "brain healthy" food, and not least, a Nintendo video game that, the instructions say, will "give your prefrontal cortex a workout." Speaking with the *Times* reporter, a spokeswoman for the American Society on Aging exclaims, "This is going to be one of the hottest topics in the next five years—it's going to be huge." Will any of it help you remember where you left your glasses, why you walked into your bedroom, or the storyline in the film you saw a few days ago? "That's the challenge," she adds. "How much science is there behind this?"

In a searing article published in the *New England Journal of Medicine*, Kate Scannell, a practicing geriatrician, decries the denial of aging that dominates our culture and argues that our refusal to accept the fact that "old age isn't just a state of mind but also a state of the body" has created a "compelling mythic structure" that not only obscures reality but is a great disservice to all of us, not just the old.

"We are regularly consumed with commercial messages that promote an experience of aging that is far more possible on billboards than in the three-dimensional lives of most elderly people," Dr. Scannell writes, as she tells the story of a seventy-six-year-old woman who came to see her, complaining that she could no longer do her usual advanced set of yoga poses without discomfort. When Dr. Scannell explained to her that "losing elasticity and flexibility with aging was a natural and regularly observed human phenomenon," the patient refused to accept the idea and insisted instead that the doctor do something. "'Well, just because that happens doesn't mean that it's healthy or inevitable, right?' she demanded. 'It's a physical process, so there must be a supplement or hormone or something physical I can take to counteract it.'"

"Our culture's compulsive spinning of old age into gold," Dr. Scannell concludes, "can inflict psycho-spiritual harm when it lures people into expecting a perpetually gilded existence, with an infomercial alchemist available at every rough and turbulent bend in the road to provide correctives that keep our lives shiny."[9] And, I might add, it hinders the development of badly needed social policies that would benefit the growing ranks of the aged. If, after all, getting old is something we can avoid, then it's not social policy that's needed to ease the problems of old age, it's personal responsibility.

In the last week alone I've read two articles, heard one radio program, and watched a TV show all proclaiming that sixty is the new forty and eighty the new sixty. Any minute I'm expecting someone out there to be redefining one hundred as advanced middle age.

Granted, given that the subject occupies my mind these days, I'm more likely than most to be tuned to it and notice every mention. But apparently it's hard for anyone to miss. An eighty-year-old friend whose body is showing serious signs of age reported with a bitter laugh that her son called one day to cheer her up with the news that he'd been watching television and heard some self-proclaimed expert talking about "the new old age."

"Can you believe it?" my friend asked. "My fifty-six-year-old son, who should know better just by looking at me these days, called to tell me that eighty is the new sixty. And I think he be-lieves it." She paused for a moment, sighed, then, "I was so irri-tated I wanted to hang up on him, then I thought, well, I guess he really needs to believe for him it will be different."

Where do these people live? I wonder. *On what planet?* It's cer-tainly true that despite all the angst about graying hair, reced-ing hairlines, expanding waistlines, sagging muscles, and failing memory, older is getting younger all the time. But sixty as the new forty?

Tell it to the fifty-five-year-old I had dinner with last night who complained that he'd had to stop running because his knees had given out.

Tell it to my friend who was looking forward to celebrating her sixtieth birthday until she got "a wake-up call" (her words, not mine) when the pain in her back was diagnosed as a degen-erative disease.

Tell it to the sixty-three-year-old who, when she heard the phrase, said bitterly, "Yeah, well two good friends died recently, and that didn't happen when I was forty."

Tell it to the fifty-nine-year-old who told me how startled he was when, during a conversation about aging, his dinner com-panion reassured him that they needn't worry about coming up on sixty. "I couldn't believe this intelligent woman really thinks that sixty is the new forty," he exclaimed. "I'd never heard it said before, and I thought she was kidding. I actually laughed, but she was really serious. I mean, sure, I know that sixty isn't what it used to be. I still have plenty of energy—well, maybe not as much as I used to have, but it's still plenty, and I can work as hard as I ever did. But it sure as hell isn't forty. At forty I didn't have the pain that's with me most of the time now. And if my body didn't re-mind me that I'm closing in on sixty, the mirror does. When I see my weathered-looking face with all its wrinkles and sags, I don't have any illusion that sixty is anything but sixty. It's different now, probably better than ever before, but still sixty."

Never mind reality; it doesn't sell. Instead we get fantasy talk about sixty being the new forty and glossy tributes to the blessings of aging. "Age has given me what I've been looking for my entire life—it gave me *me*," exclaims the writer Anne Lamott. "It provided the time and experience and failures and triumphs and friends who helped me step into the shape that had been waiting for me all my life."

Would she give it up for thinner thighs or a flatter belly? On her bad days, perhaps, but mostly her answer is: "Are you crazy?"

Sounds great, no? Who can argue with the experience of growing into a self you like and respect? Who would say it isn't one of the gifts of getting older? But she was forty-nine when she wrote those words, middle-aged by today's definition, and coming to terms with oneself is what that life stage is all about. As I write today, a forty-nine-year-old can expect to inhabit this middle stage for the next fifteen or twenty years and, if she's lucky, healthy, and open to the experience, these can be vital, growing years.

But then comes "the new old age," when Ms. Lamott and her peers will confront the next twenty or thirty years and giving up thinner thighs is the least of their worries. "Every one of my friends loves being older," she enthuses. "My Aunt Gertrude is eighty-five and leaves us behind in the dust when we hike." Maybe so, but I wonder how Aunt Gertrude feels when she goes home alone to nurse her sore muscles, eat her solitary dinner, and count up her losses that lie next to the pleasure of the hike.

It's time for something more, something besides our fantasies and denials, something besides the one-sided media representations about all the ways of being old that are supposedly open to us now: the seventy-six-year-old who runs the Boston Marathon in respectable time, the eighty-five-year-old who plays a mean game of tennis every day, the former president who parachutes from a plane to celebrate his eightieth birthday, the eighty-one-year-old who climbs El Capitan in Yosemite, the ninety-two-year-old who still has an eye for the women and the wherewithal to do something about it, the eighty-two-year-old who sells her first painting.

I know these possibilities. I am the eighty-two-year-old who sold that painting. And I know the complex of feeling and fear that drives people to such adventures in their old age, the deep-seated need for something to give meaning to a life, the illusion that if we climb one more mountain we can control not just life but death as well.

Like Aunt Gertrude, I love it when I can match or best a younger companion in the outdoors, or when I see some fifty-year-old huffing and puffing on his treadmill at the gym when I haven't broken a real sweat. But these are transient moments of triumph that live next to the more permanent realizations about the diminishing self that old age brings.

This isn't to say that the heroic feats of the old don't deserve celebration, that they aren't useful in offering up an image of what may be possible. But while we applaud, it's well to remember that it's the rare person at any age, let alone old age, who has the will or the wherewithal—whether internal resources or financial freedom—to even think about climbing mountains and jumping from planes.

What's more, when the media turn their attention to other excitements and our fifteen minutes of fame has passed, we're left alone to contemplate the reality that, no matter how inspiring the accomplishment, no matter how much notice it gets, having achieved the goal we still face the question that haunts all of us who are confronting a very long old age: "Now what?"

Yes, "Now what?" That's the big question no one is asking.

What if those scientists working in their labs actually find the key to the fountain of youth? What if we could live to 125? How will we live those years? What will we do with them? What will sustain us—emotionally, economically, physically, spiritually? Who will we become? These, not just whether the old will break the Social Security bank, are the central questions about aging in our time.

Chapter Three

Staying Younger While Getting Older

Staying younger while getting older—sounds like an oxymoron, doesn't it, puzzling in its contradictions. Yet this is what aging is in this early part of the twenty-first century. Not for everyone, of course. Some people still die at sixty, some are infirm at seventy, and more than a few live with an assortment of aches, pains, and illnesses that don't allow any illusions about staying younger. But what makes this time so interesting—and problematic—is that most of us *are* staying younger while getting older. Not just living longer, but looking better, feeling better, living better than ever before.

Standing alone, that's little more than an interesting observation. Put it in the context of the social world in which we live and it becomes a remarkable fact, one that demands our closest public and private attention. For it isn't only the old who are affected by a life that, like the Energizer Bunny, keeps going and going. This single demographic fact ricochets around the society like a shot fired in an echo chamber, undergirding the most important social and cultural changes of our time and revolutionizing the public sphere as well as the private one.

It's axiomatic that cultures change in response to changing social conditions. The demographic reality of an era is inevitably reflected in the development of new social norms and roles. As the content of socialization changes in the external world, the psychology of our internal world shifts as well. Suddenly, formerly unseen possibilities for living come into view.

So it is that throughout history the very concepts of childhood, adolescence, adulthood, and old age—and the cultural norms that accompany these life stages—have been shaped, at least in part, by the length of the life span. In the seventeenth century when forty was advanced old age, there was little thought to the special needs of childhood, and the idea of adolescence didn't exist. There was only youth and old age, with a few years in between for bearing and raising the next generation. Children were often betrothed just out of infancy, married in their early teens, and bore their own children as quickly as their bodies would allow. Now, it's hard to imagine sending our thirteen-year-olds into marriage. Then, when death commonly came by the mid-thirties and forty was old age, it was the only way to ensure the continuity of generations.

It took the excesses of the Industrial Revolution of the mid-eighteenth century to make childhood as "childhood" noticeable. I don't mean that children weren't cared for, valued, and even loved before that time. But their value was likely to be connected to what they could contribute in the family, whether to its economic needs in the present or in providing care for their parents in the future, rather than just because they existed.

As children as young as six, sometimes accompanied by their mothers, sometimes not, left the fields of their fathers to work in the factories of the cities, they came into public view. Until then, children, even abused children, were "family business," not a matter for public concern. With their entry into the world of working adults, they came to be seen as individuals separate from the family unit, little ones to be sure, but nevertheless workers who earned wages, were subject to an authority other than their parents and were therefore an appropriate object of public attention. As reformers of the era brought the deplorable conditions in the factories into public awareness—children cruelly exploited, chained to machines for fourteen and more hours a day and beaten when they dropped—the idea of childhood as a stage of life deserving of special protection was born.

Adolescence would wait until advancing technology changed the requirements for industrial workers. By the mid-nineteenth century, the technology of the factory floor had changed sufficiently so that a pair of willing hands was no longer enough to get and hold a job. The burgeoning industries now required educated skills to guide the hands. Advanced public education—meaning something beyond elementary school—was the answer.

Thus was adolescence "discovered," fed by the twin needs of the economy and society. Industry needed educated workers. The cities and towns that emerged when farmers-turned-workers flooded into the factories found themselves dealing with the threat of roving bands of unschooled and unskilled young people who, as the factories became more mechanized, now had nothing to do. The public high school seemed to offer a solution to both problems.[1]

Like all social innovations, however, it had unintended consequences. As these schools took shape across the land, they created the social setting in which teenagers came together for the first time and, in the process, eventually welded themselves into the kind of peer group culture we know today. Adolescence as a distinct stage of life was born and given form in the halls of America's high schools.

In our own time, we have seen extraordinary changes in the meaning of each of these life stages. Children, once valued as necessary contributors to the family economy, are now the cosseted, protected fodder for what Diane Ehrensaft calls "expect-able parental narcissism"[2]—a phenomenon that has become ac-ceptable and "expectable" only in the last few decades.

Adolescence, once defined as a haven for children between thirteen and eighteen, has now expanded its parameters into the twenties and beyond partly because the changes in the economy wrought by the post–Industrial Revolution demand a new kind of work force. As the manufacturing and industrial sectors of the economy continue to shrink, new skills are required to meet the needs of the expanding service and technology sectors. A high school diploma, once the ticket to a job that had at least the prospect of a living wage, one that could support a family, a car, and a modest house, is no longer enough. College now serves the function high school once did. It offers training and skills while keeping the young occupied and off the streets until industry and society find a place for them.

Presently, about one-quarter of our young people have at least some college. Since even those students who also hold jobs usually can't manage without additional financial help, it means that someone is paying at least part of the bill, whether through grants, loans, or parental beneficence. And that, in turn, means that post-teeners who would have been working and self-supporting in earlier times remain in a dependent, adolescent state for years.

But the needs of the economy are only one part of the story. For the other part, we have to look to our increasingly long life span, which is the bedrock on which the shift in the boundaries of our various life stages stands. I don't mean we wake up one morning and say, "Hey, now that I'll probably live to be eighty, I don't have to get married at twenty anymore." Or that we're con-scious of what motivates our changing ideas about the timing and sequencing of major life events. Rather, the reality of our ex-panded life, a reality observed even when it doesn't fully enter conscious thought, infuses all of us with a new and enlarged sense of life's possibilities and opportunities. Suddenly work, family, identity—all these and more are up for discussion as the new demographics give rise to a changing culture that alters our vision of the possible. We grow up later, marry later, have children later, stay on the job longer than ever before. Everything changes, all because the years stretch so far ahead.

If at eighteen you see your older siblings and their friends marrying for the first time in their late twenties, becoming parents in their mid-thirties, your grandparents alive and functioning at seventy-five, it's hard to feel any immediate urgency about growing up, getting married, having children.

"My parents want me to go to college now, but why?" asks a seventeen-year-old high school senior. "I mean, I've been in school like my whole life; I want to do something else for a while. Like travel or maybe, you know, get a job in another country. I mean, yeah, I want to go to college, I do. I know I have to. But, geez, I got my whole life ahead of me. So what if I go to college next year, or even five years from now. Like, you know, I mean, what's the hurry?"

If the economy that supported your parents into the middle class and above no longer holds out the promise of a decent job at a living wage, let alone one that will provide their level of affluence and a home of your own, why not retain your identification with the youth culture as long as you can?[3]

"I know you think I'm supposed to be a serious adult now that I've graduated from college, but that's only because you're not the one looking for a job," remarks an unemployed twenty-two-year-old. "You know, you do everything you're supposed to do, I mean, like you go to college and get decent grades. Then you get out and there's shit jobs waiting for you. So you live with your parents and wait for something to break, and, you know, hang out with the guys just like before. My parents keep nagging me to grow up, but

I don't know, I mean, I don't see a lot of advantage in being an adult."

If working for the rest of your life means doing the same thing for sixty years, maybe beginning later is a better idea anyway.

"Hey, I look at my dad; he's like fifty-seven years old and he's been working at the same job for *thirty-three years* [emphasis his], and he'll be doing it until he dies," says an eighteen-year-old recent high-school graduate who has been arguing with his parents about his plans for the future. "So what's the hurry about going to college and getting a job? I mean, for what? So I can do the same thing for fifty years?"

"What's the hurry?"—words that run like a refrain through my conversations with young people. Their parents, having themselves broken through the norms of their time and knowing the gains, the losses, and the unpredictability of life, are ambivalent. They have some sympathy with their children's view, even agree in some ways and encourage it, but they worry about pushing the boundaries too far, fearful of roads not taken and opportunities missed. So they push the children along, not exactly to stay in the traditional pattern of the life course, but not getting too far off it either: Get educated first, then go off and do what you want. Don't take the first job that comes along, but you have to start somewhere. Don't get married too young, but what are you waiting for? Don't rush to have children, but remember the clock is ticking. But their children, coming of age in a world where life seems to stretch into eternity, can only ask, "What's the hurry?"

As the years that define adolescence multiply, ideas about adulthood change as well. Until recently, marriage was the entry point into adulthood, a milestone people sought. That's no longer so. When people live to eighty and beyond, definitions of adulthood become more fluid, and choices that were unavailable, even unthinkable before, now lie before them.

There's no longer any social necessity for people to marry in their teens to ensure that they'll live long enough to launch the next generation. Nor is there any psychological imperative to rush into marriage when the years extend so far ahead and when, at the same time, the privileges of adulthood that once went with marriage alone are now readily available to singles as well.

"Sure, I want to get married and have kids one day, but there's no rush," explains an attractive twenty-four-year-old woman who works as a hostess in an upscale restaurant. "I mean, I've got this job I like, I've got friends and a boyfriend. I don't want a husband now. I mean, what I want right now is a little more money in my paycheck, and I'll get that soon. I'm after the assistant manager's job, and I think I'll get it. I'm just not ready to give all this up to become a wife and mother."

In the past, people married, bore children, and came to midlife at roughly the same age and stage, which made the markers of middle age easy to define. But no more. Take age, for example. When I wrote about midlife women in the late 1970s, the lower end of the age range was thirty-five, the upper end fifty-four.[4] Now thirty-five seems much too young to define the beginning of middle age and sixty-five has barely seen the end of it.

We can't easily define midlife by life stage anymore either. Not when one forty-five-year-old woman is inching toward grandmotherhood, while her next-door neighbor is clutching her pregnant belly as she chases after her two-year-old. Or when one fifty-five-year-old man is coaching his seven-year-old's soccer team, while the guy who works at the next desk is thinking about retirement now that he's just seen his last child leave home.

Such variations leave the experts scratching their heads about where to set the boundaries of middle age. In the real world, it makes no difference what they decide; we know it when we see it. Or perhaps I should say feel it.

In a recent *New York Times* article titled "Fatherhood, I Now Learn, Is a Young Man's Game," a forty-six-year-old first-time father writes: "Already I was feeling pretty creaky, the consequence of a nasty basketball habit I couldn't kick. Ankle sprains, back spasms and, finally, the mother of all sports injuries, a torn anterior cruciate ligament. . . . Will I have the energy to be an older father? The patience? The knees?" he asks.

He found out just how hard it would be on his new family's first day home from the hospital: "I bent over to take an ice tray from the freezer, when, wham! Someone kicked a dagger-toed boot into my lower back. I went down, ice trays flying. These were the same back spasms that felled me on the basketball court a year ago. I couldn't get up, couldn't even sit up."[5]

Most people probably aren't quite so "creaky" at forty-six, but the body sends its messages in other ways as well. A couple of weeks ago a fifty-five-year-old friend who recently left a job as a corporate executive for one that doesn't require the long hours and, in his words, the "brain strain," called to complain about the change.

"Why did you leave your other job?" I asked.

"I've thought a lot about that," he replied, "and I think it was more than I wanted to do. I don't have the same manic drive I used to have."

"Do you think that has something to do with moving along in your fifties?"

"No," he said, a bit too quickly. A moment of silence, then, as if he had just heard his words, "Well, I don't know. Now you're asking me to think about it on another level. I'm just saying what comes immediately to mind, and that's that I tire more easily."

"And you don't think that has to do with your age?"

"Yeah, well, I guess now that you push me on it. It's like you lose some resiliency and don't bounce back like you used to. You can't concentrate as deeply for so long, so the work feels harder. I'd get tired before, but it was different. Now there's a kind of exhaustion that leaks into other parts of my life and that made it untenable to continue to do that kind of work."

It's a conversation I've had over the years with dozens of middle-aged women and men who were surprised to find themselves feeling the weight of their bodies in unaccustomed ways. Suddenly it seems, the body sags, the waist thickens, flesh droops, bulges appear where they never existed before, memory slips, something hurts today that wasn't a problem yesterday.

They talk about it, agonize about it, laugh about it as they try to find ways to accept the inevitability of their own decline. But the sadness is there, lurking beneath the surface of daily life as surely as tomorrow comes. "I'm finding that middle age isn't so easy to come to terms with, either," writes a fifty-year-old friend. "Fading beauty. Achy joints. And I gather that it's not going to get better as things go on."

I was having lunch a few days ago with a fifty-four-year-old colleague when she was visited by one of those middle-age moments of awareness. We were speaking of books we'd read, and I recommended one I'd just finished. "My memory is terrible these days," she said, searching in her purse for a pen and notepad. "I don't even try to remember anymore; I just write everything down."

"How long has that been going on?" I asked.

Without a moment's hesitation, she replied, "I don't remember."

Her words stopped us both in midbreath and a split-second look of sadness crossed her face before we burst out laughing at the absurdity of life and what it visits on us.

Whatever our capacity for denial, however hard we work to retain at least the illusion of youth, by the time we reach those middle years, we know somewhere inside that we have come to that turning that signals its loss. And we know also, perhaps for the first time, the inevitability of our mortality. Physically we can't easily deny the signals of aging our body sends; psychologically we wrestle with the conflicts of this oddly contradictory period in our lives. Reflecting on his awakening sense of life's limits, a fifty-eight-year-old friend writes, "The moments are neither infinite nor finite—and we find ourselves suspended somewhere between the midst and the mist, seeking the sun, but aware of the fog, not counting the days, but measuring the seasons."

This is the paradox of middle age. It is both the high noon of life, the time when we stand at the pinnacle, while our very position there forces us into facing the reality of the losses to come. It's a time when doors both open and close, when everything seems possible and nothing does; a time when we take pleasure in knowing we're at the top of our game, while confronting the painful realization that it's downhill from there. It's a time of reckoning, of celebration as we consolidate life's gains, and torment as we confront our losses, a time of growth and decline, of a renewed search for meaning, both personal and existential, a time of endings and beginnings that's a confusing blend of hope and sorrow.

Chapter Four

Does Age Count Anymore?

If middle age is the high noon of life, old age is its sunset. Like the other stages of life these days, where it begins isn't easily marked, but the end is the one utterly predictable event in a life filled with unpredictability.

In earlier times chronological age often was irrelevant. Most people didn't really know how old they were; birth records, when they existed, were inscribed in the church or synagogue and dependent on whether the record keeper was faithful to the task. My mother, who was born in pre–World War I Russia, had only a hazy idea of her age and made up a birth date when she came through Ellis Island only because the customs agent asked for it.

It's still true in most preliterate societies today. Everyone knows when someone has lived a long time, of course; the evidence is visible in every line on the face. But unlike our own culture with its glorification of youth, the elders wear those lines comfortably, for they are the signs of wisdom, the visible reminders that the old are the carriers of the community's history. In such societies "old" is when a person becomes dependent, can't work anymore, or can't keep up with the tribe's movements. When that happens, when, in essence, the old have served their purpose, passed on what they know, the community culture can often be no kinder than ours: the old are left behind to die.

But here, as in most Western industrialized societies, the various phases of life are marked by chronological age. So when does old age happen? Even the demographers and gerontologists keep changing their minds about what marks old age. They used to call sixty-five old, now some think of it as advanced middle age. Then it was seventy-five that became the marker for old. But that didn't work for long, so they moved it up to eighty. Oops! Not that either. The only thing left was to split "old" into new categories. Sixty-five to seventy-four became the "young old," while seventy-five to eighty-four is now the "old old." What to do with the over eighty-fives? That's easy. We make them the "oldest old."

Well, not so easy, since not everyone agrees that these are the right categories. It will no doubt pain most fifty-five-year-olds to hear that some social gerontologists lump them with the young old along with the seventy-four-year-olds, a couple of whom might well be their parents. And still others, not satisfied with only three categories of old, have come up with a fourth: "middle old." As far as I can tell, though, no one is entirely sure who fits into it.

But even those modifications were not enough to suit some of the experts who work in the field, so we now have a whole new set of classifications of the old, one that fits more neatly into our cultural abhorrence of old age by abjuring the word "old" entirely. There's the "Third Age," an ever-evolving category that, depending on who's defining it, is either a rough and open-ended expansion upward of the young old, or one that includes everyone from fifty on. But since we're living so long these days, some analysts have concluded that we need a "Fourth Age," which is somewhat equivalent to the oldest old—that is, everyone over eighty-five.

"The idea of the Third and Fourth Age itself is undergoing change and strictly speaking is not tied to a specific age range," write Paul Baltes and Jacqui Smith. "Rather...[they] are dynamic and moving targets that are themselves subject to evolution and variation."[1] Which means in plain English that these are more concepts than categories, that they define an idea—the Third Age being "the big success story" of our time as exemplified by the dramatic increase in longevity whose end point we don't yet know; the Fourth Age marked by physical and mental frailty. As the number of people over one hundred, already mushrooming at a rapid rate, continues to rise, the categorizers will no doubt be back at their drawing boards. Will there be a Fifth Age? Stay tuned.

Whatever the issues and merits of each of these different kinds of classifications, the shift in thinking from the traditional age-related distinctions to something less fixed, more fluid, makes sense to me. For when we situate our old into firm chronological categories, it obscures the great variability in how individuals age, doesn't easily take account of the eighty-year-olds who are running all over town and the sixty-year-olds who can't make it to the corner store.

Unfortunately, however, the new categories don't provide much more light than the old ones. If frailty, whether physical or mental, is the defining feature separating the Third from the Fourth Age, it means we'd have to put the ninety-year-old who still functions well on both counts into the same category as the sixty-five-year-olds. Not something that makes sense in the real world, no matter how well a ninety-year-old may be holding up.

Which leads me to ask: What is it that makes it so hard to keep two thoughts in our minds at the same time? Why do we have to think in opposites, one side against the other? Variation exists among the old, perhaps more so than in other groups —and so do commonalities. If we insist on variability as the singular defining factor, we leave ourselves with nothing to say, since every generalization we make about old age—what it is, when it happens, how people feel about it—will be contradicted by those individuals who don't fit the pattern. The task, then, is to find the path between the individual and the general, some place where our analysis recognizes variation but also leaves us able to make general statements.

My husband, who just turned ninety, doesn't like being old any better than I do, but he handles it with a graceful acceptance I doubt I'll ever manage. I stamp my foot and rage at fate because his memory is failing, his mind losing its edge. He's saddened by what's happening to him, gets momentarily frustrated when he can't remember how to do some simple task, but ultimately comes down on the side of, "I'm lucky to be able to do as well as I can." I push against the limits, grumble about getting tired when I didn't before, about not being able to walk as far or as long as I could a few years ago. He smiles and says, "But look how far you can still walk."

I don't want to hear his reassurance; I want to shake him, make him join me in my angry resistance. He wishes I'd calm down, be quiet, and let him enjoy his time in peace. But the differences in how we manage the day-to-day pressures of getting old fade into insignificance when compared to the shared experience of what it *means* to get old, our mutual understanding of the painful and difficult realities of this time of life.

My argument, then, is that alongside the variability lie deeply felt commonalities that bind people of a similar age together no matter how different they may appear on the outside or how their temperaments may vary. I saw it in live action during one recent holiday weekend when I went to a block party with people ranging from two months to ninety years and watched similar-aged people come together like homing pigeons. Never mind that some sixty-year-olds looked ten years older and some ten years younger; never mind that a couple of seventy-five-year-olds looked older than my ninety-year-old husband. They were bound together by the common experiences of their age and life stage. The sixty-year-olds were preoccupied with retaining their youthful vigor at the same time they were wondering whether it was time to slow down, to "cut back." Those fifteen and twenty years ahead of them were discussing, among other aging problems, the difficulties of already having cut back or having been cut out altogether.

True, I'm especially sensitive to such conversations these days, and I probably encouraged them, eager as I am to hear what people have to say. But I didn't push anyone into the subject; I just listened to what was already being said and made a remark or asked a question when the opportunity presented itself.

I see it also in my responses and reactions to the people I meet in this work—and theirs to me. Although we're strangers when we meet, I soon find myself feeling an affinity with them, a kind of oneness that goes even deeper than empathy, something that resides in the core of our mutual understanding about the trials of old age, a bonding that comes with recognizing so many of their thoughts as my own, the knowledge that, even with those who experience this stage of life with greater ease than I do, there's an understanding that transcends the differences.

There are, of course, important differences among the old as well, differences that separate them by virtue of class, culture, ethnicity, and gender. A woman who lives on the edge of poverty worries about money in ways that I do not. A person embedded in a large, extended Latino family will be less lonely, less isolated than a white counterpart whose children are on the other side of the country. A single man, no matter how old, what he looks like, or what his physical condition, is more likely to find female companionship than a healthy and attractive sixty-five-year-old single woman is to have a man in her life.

Temperament, too, makes a difference. Some people accept the trials of aging philosophically, some don't. Some, the lucky ones with the will, the resources, and the talent, make a new and satisfying life for themselves, while others feel cheated and mourn the past. A man who has morphed from corporate executive into a sculptor and feels free for the first time in his life has a whole different set of experiences from the one who mourns the loss of his earlier self and has been unable to find a new one.

It seems easy to label the differences among us. Some people are resigned, some depressed, some accepting, some content with this time of life. But such labels don't do justice to the complex and contradictory sets of feelings that live inside us. They sing the lyrics, not the melody, play the movement, not the symphony.

A friend tells me that she feels good, sometimes even happy, with the life she's made as a widow at eighty, and speaks of the pleasures of being able to live these years unfettered by the ambitions and internal strife that dominated her before. Even though I haven't found her level of acceptance, I know what she means: the relief in giving up the strivings, the moments of pure pleasure in a beautiful sunset, the smell of the ocean, the smile of a great-grandchild—moments that passed before you could savor them fully when you had to move on to the next thing. Physically, however, we switch places. She worries about every new pain, rushes off to the doctor hoping she'll tell her it's not serious and make it go away. I take them as they come, assuming that they're the natural accompaniment of old age. Which of us is resistant, which accepting?

No matter what label we affix, when we look more closely we see that the resigned also resist, the depressed know joy, the accepting struggle, the content are well acquainted with unhappiness. And more. Whatever the variations in temperament and experience that make for differences among the old, we all share the fundamental social and personal difficulties that go with being old, we all know those periods of despair when the pain of aging outweighs everything else.

But, one might ask: What's different here? Isn't there plenty of reason for unhappiness, even despair, at other stages of life? Yes. Ask any adolescent. Life is, in fact, a series of gains and losses, and every beginning foreshadows an ending. But until now, whatever sadness the ending may have generated, whatever sense of loss it brought, was balanced by the promise the beginning held out, the promise of a new adventure, of a time when some part of the world opens up. We move from child to adult and give up the protection and safety of childhood for the privileges of adulthood. The children leave home and we're saddened by the loss of their voices in the house, the sound of their feet on the steps. But we also see freedom ahead, freedom from the many constraints parenthood imposes, an opening up of new possibilities for living. Not a bad exchange for missing their steps on the stair.

What's the trade-off in old age? Yes, we have wisdom, but how often are we called upon to offer it up? Yes, we have time, but for most of us the question is: Time for what? For all the things we couldn't do before, we say. But what happens when we have too much time? No one, perhaps, has answered the question more eloquently than Philip Roth in his moving tale of an aging "everyman": "Suddenly," he writes, "he was lost in nothing, in the sound of the two syllables 'nothing' no less than in the nothingness, lost and drifting, and dread began to seep in."[2] A voice of truth for all the old folks who spend their days listlessly before the TV screen hardly knowing or caring what's playing, grateful for some distraction, for a voice in the house to ease the loneliness and boredom. "TV is the only friend I've got left," an eighty-nine-year-old woman tells me as she reaches for the remote so we can talk without the background noise.

"So," asks a friend with whom I'd been talking about some of these issues, "is there a time you'd like to go back to?" The answer comes easily, since I already know that, much as I'm troubled by what it means to get old in this society, I don't want to go back to some earlier period. I'm wiser today than I was twenty years ago, and in many ways, more satisfied with who I am, more at ease with myself and my life. I don't want to return to some earlier period and give up what I've gained. I don't ever again want to be too busy to appreciate the small, joyful moments of life. I just wish I could have it all, that I could know what I know today, be who I am now, and live in the world as I did twenty years ago, when it and I still had room for each other, when I didn't have to face the knowledge that the society I live in has little use for me, when I felt *in* the world, an active participant rather than an onlooker. A fantasy I'm certain no old person would reject.

My nostalgic wish to be both who I am now and who I was then must sound anomalous to another's ears, perhaps even implausible, since I'm the one writing this book, an act that in itself puts me in the world. But a single act, a special moment, wonderful and important though it may be, doesn't change the realities of being old in America, doesn't erase the stigma of age—not how society views us, not how we view ourselves.

Yes, I know, age, like beauty, is said to be in the eye of the beholder. But the beholder's eye sees both age and beauty in a cultural context. The French anthropologist Claude Lévi-Strauss reports that the Nambikwara Indians have a single word that means "young and beautiful" and another that means "old and ugly."[3] Scarification is the mark of beauty in some cultures; to us a scar is something to hide. Old age may be venerated in some places—at least so long as the old continue to have some use;

we're repelled by it, offended, want to push it out of our sight and our consciousness.

I know, too, that our view of old age depends on where we are in the life cycle. When we were children, old was our thirty-year-old parents and *really* old was our fifty-year-old grandparents. When I turned sixty, it seemed old to me. Now that I'm past eighty and my daughter is closing in on sixty, it's young. But that doesn't change that I know I'm old, even if I also know that if I live to one hundred—not something I long for, to be honest—I'll be older still.

One of the hopeful myths about aging is that you're as old as you feel, meaning that your psychological state, the attitudes you bring to getting old, affect how well or badly you manage it. Or as Satchel Paige, the famous African American baseball player, quipped, "Age is a question of mind over matter. If you don't mind, it doesn't matter."

It's a glib remark, effortlessly tossed off, and like all clichés it holds a core of truth. But it doesn't say much, since I can't think of any issue we might face in life where it's not true. If we tend toward the depressive side, whatever we confront will probably feel worse than it is; if we're of a more sunny disposition, it will almost surely look better.

That said, I must also say: *Age counts.* Not in the fixed and firm way the traditional categories suggest; not in the same way it counted a half century ago. But it counts both in the external world and in the internal one—in the society, in the body, and in the mind.

Socially, old age is still an abomination. Too strong a word? Maybe. But ask yourself when was the last time you looked at someone who's old, maybe who shuffles a bit when he walks, without a shudder, without wanting to look away, without thinking you're glad that's not you. Ask yourself when was the last time you sought out the company of someone twenty or thirty years older than you are, not as some obligation to your old parents or grandparents, not as a way to soothe your conscience about your negative feelings by spending an hour in an old-age home at Christmas, but because you really like that person and think she has something to say that will interest you.

Friends and colleagues with whom I've talked about the social stigma of aging almost invariably tell me that this is the curse of modern industrial society and wax eloquent about how preindustrial cultures honor and revere their elders. I know the stories; I once believed them myself—and sometimes they're even true. But as with everything else about the subject of aging, the reverence of the old in those societies is only one part of the story. When we look beyond our own nostalgic fantasy for another, better time and place, we find that honor often holds only so long as the old have something to offer, whether as productive members of the community or the repositories of the social and cultural history.

Take their folklore, for example. There we see a view of the old stripped of the romantic haze that has infused many of our own anthropological studies. In an extensive compilation of the folklore of aging ranging across various cultures and several centuries, D. L. Ashliman, professor emeritus of German and folklorist at the University of Pittsburgh, presents an illuminating and vivid tale of the bitterness of old age—a tale of community ambivalence at best, distrust and revulsion at worst—from which few, if any, societies seem to be exempt.

> For most pre-industrial cultures, life's last chapter has been a bitter one. Surviving folklore reflects widespread resignation as to the inevitability of impoverishment, sexual impotence, failing health and vitality, and the loss of family and community sta-

tus.... In spite of the numerous tales and proverbs celebrating the wisdom of old people and promoting their care, folklore is replete with reflections of a basic distrust of age.[4]

Proverbs tell both sides of the story: "He who does not honor age does not deserve age" and "An old man can see backward better than a young one can see forward" stand alongside "Nothing good will come from an old man who still wants to dance" and "Good deeds are wasted on old men and on rogues."

Notice, though, that the positive side refers only to men. When it comes to women, ambivalence recedes behind the belief that they have evil powers and bring bad luck: "If the devil can't come himself, he sends an old woman." "He who walks between two old women early in the morning shall have only bad luck the rest of the day." In these societies, many men, according to Ashliman, would rather let themselves get beaten to death than to pass between two old women.

Caring for old parents was apparently no less a burden in preindustrial societies than in our own. The most widely known story is the Eskimo compact between the old and the young. When it was time for the tribe to move, those who had outlived their usefulness and couldn't keep up the pace set by the young willingly stayed behind to perish in the snow rather than risk the safety of the entire community. But Ashliman presents plenty of other evidence to show that, in the words of one folk saying, "The parent's death is often the children's good fortune," and that neglect, ritual killings, euthanasia, and geronticide were widespread.

From the Greeks to the present time, old age has been met with attitudes ranging from ambivalence to abhorrence. True, the Greeks revered the image of the Homeric sage, but in everyday life, they extolled the glories of youth and beauty, believed it was a duty to keep "him who is unable to live well from living ill," and often used hemlock to poison those over sixty.[5] Nor is there a shortage in Greek literature of imagery that depicts the old with disgust. Sophocles portrays the aged Oedipus as "disappraised, infirm, unsociable, unfriended, with whom all woe of woe abides."[6] Aristotle speaks of old age as the "demon" that robs men of their physical and moral spirit.

Early Christian tradition, too, has its share of imagery that speaks to the ugliness of the physical and moral decline of the old. "For like elderly men who have no hope of renewing their strength, and expect nothing but their last sleep, so you, weakened by worldly occupations, have given yourselves up to sloth," lectures the Pastor of Hermas.[7] And Augustine, perhaps the most influential theologian in Christendom, writes, "When life draws to a close, the old man is full of complaint, and with no joys . . . groans abound even unto the decrepitude of old age."[8] As with the Greeks, this dim view isn't the whole story of attitudes toward the old in Christian tradition, but it does represent a strong current that runs through centuries of literature.

Western literature, with its exaggerated reverence for youth, is shot through with references to the beauty of the young compared to the ugliness of the old. Echoing the chorus of those who came before him, the French philosopher Montaigne excoriates the old as filled with "envy, injustice, and malice," and goes on to say: "Age imprints more wrinkles in the mind than it does on the face; and souls are never, or even rarely seen, that in growing old do not smell sour and musty."[9]

What do you feel when you read those words? Do you cringe, think *Not me*, remember the time when you looked at an old person and thought something very much like this, changed your seat on the subway or bus so as not to get too close, as if he had a communicable disease?

In our time we know better than to say such things; it's not politically correct. But withholding the words doesn't silence the thoughts, any more than banishing "old" from our vocabulary in favor of "senior citizen" has had any substantial impact on either our social or personal attitudes about the old.

In *The Fountain of Age*, Betty Friedan cites a Harris Poll finding that most people over sixty-five resist euphemisms like "senior citizen" or "mature Americans" almost as much as they do terms like "old," "older Americans," and even "retired Americans."[10] Which suggests that they understand all too well that there is currently no language in this society that will reduce the stigma of age and, therefore, none that the old will wear comfortably.

It's not that a change in language isn't helpful in changing perception, just that it can happen only when the new words rest in changed cultural understandings. For language and culture live in reciprocal relationship to each other, and a change in one is likely to bring a shift in the other. So, for example, each change in the way we refer to black Americans—from "colored" to "Negro" to "black" to "African American"—made some difference because it rested on changing cultural norms brought about by decades of struggle that culminated in the Civil Rights Movement of the 1950s and early 1960s. Feminism, too, changed not just the language but the cultural landscape within which women lived and, not least, the public understandings of the very meaning of the word "woman." Until ageism comes under the same kind of public scrutiny with a political movement to match, euphemisms like "senior citizen" will be met with disdain by both the old and the society in which they live.

Chapter Five

The Marriage
of Self and Society

When I was a graduate student, the dominant sociological theory about aging rested on something called "disengagement theory," the basic assumption of which was that healthy aging required people to disengage from meaningful life activities. It's natural, these theorists argued, that the old would choose to disengage from active participation in society—natural for the person and beneficial to the society.

Natural? Well, maybe. It's certainly true that the older we get, the more likely we are to be ready to free ourselves from the constraints of the roles we've inhabited for so long, to withdraw, to husband our strength and our energy. We know what mountains we've conquered, what we couldn't do, and the lucky among us are satisfied with what we see. It's time to step back, to reflect on our lives, on who we were, who we've become and how we got there; time also to find a way toward a future that's not immediately apparent, and, paradoxically, to plan for life while preparing also to leave it.

So, yes, disengagement theorists got some things right, but they also got a lot wrong. For one thing, they assumed that because the old are no longer considered useful in society, it's natural for them to choose to opt out, forgetting or ignoring how much of engagement and disengagement is an interactive process. When society has no use for some segment of its people, when their presence is an inconvenience, an embarrassment, or simply undesired, people of any age will disengage.

Stereotypes that dog our steps—whether based on race, age, or gender—are powerful disincentives to engagement, to say nothing of how destructive they are to the soul. We see it in the significant numbers of young black men who have disengaged, sometimes because they're so angry, but often because it's the only way they can figure out to preserve some positive sense of self. And we see it among the old who more and more close themselves off in the euphemistically labeled "active adult communities," homogeneous residential facilities where, because they're surrounded by others like themselves, they're insulated from the stigma that accompanies them in the world outside.[1]

Listen to the voices of those who live in such communities and you'll hear them speak about the comfort of being with age peers, the sense of belonging and acceptance, the easy companionship, the planned activities designed to meet their needs and interests. "We're all in the same boat. It's a nice feeling; it's a very congenial group," is the way one woman puts it.

Disengagement theory has always had its critics, and their voices have grown louder as our longer life has brought the issues of the old into greater public awareness. But as is true in many parts of American life, whether social or scientific, the new heedlessly sweeps out the old. So the theory of disengagement has been discarded in favor of a new one that foresees a life of endless engagement—a view of aging that's as one-sided as the old one was.

For like everything else about old age, it's not all or nothing, not disengagement or engagement, but both forces working inside us all the time: the pull of disengagement that feels like preparation for what is inevitably our future, a subtle pulling away, an inwardness that wants solitude and keeps us from entering the social world as fully as we did before; the push toward engagement that seeks to give meaning to the present while delaying the future, the wish to be seen, to be heard, to be counted, to be needed.

How, then, does one find meaning in a society where dignity and respect are so closely associated with work and productivity? We need to engage a spiritual quest, some people say, the search for something inside that is perhaps truer, deeper, more transcendent than the life we've lived until now. I'm never quite sure what that means. Friends who are practicing Buddhists speak of finding the way to balance the physical with the spiritual, of living and experiencing the present moment fully, with no comparison, no judgment, no thought of anything else, of leaving behind the strivings we all know to discover something more fundamental inside us, something closer to our essential self.

Certainly, it's possible to free ourselves from some of the most destructive effects of our competitive, production-oriented society. Sure, we can live in the moment—for a moment. But how can this be a way of life when, because we have the gift of memory and consciousness, we bring every moment we've lived into every moment we're living? And what about this essential self people speak of? Is there really such a thing, a self that exists outside of past experience and free of society's norms and values?

Perhaps my doubts flow from my sociological training, perhaps from my thirty-five years of experience as a psychotherapist, perhaps it's simple truth. We, all of us, live in a dynamic interactive process with the world around us. The social world changes, and so do we. Just forty years ago marriage between blacks and whites was illegal in many states; today most of us consider such restrictions unthinkable. Until then, too, states had the right to outlaw contraceptive use, even in marriage, an idea so at odds with our beliefs now that we wonder how it could ever have been acceptable.

We take on a new role—worker, wife, husband, mother, father—and grow into it, changing and broadening what until then was the self we knew. It doesn't always happen easily and without conflict, but if we live the role long enough, it becomes part of who we are, even after we have left it. A husband dies and the part of his widow that was his wife remains alive inside her. How could it be otherwise when the experience of that marriage is an integral part of the self she knows?

This isn't to say we're little more than lumps of clay to be molded into the shape society prefers. Rather, my argument is that from birth onward we are active and seeking participants in our development—seeking, in that we continually respond to our internal need for connection with another; active, in that we are in a constant process of internalizing representations of people and objects from the world around us. A sense of self and personal identity is formed and sharpened in the context of such social interaction, products of the interplay between the external and the internal, between social experience and its psychological elaboration. It's the power of these socializing forces that welds us into a society of people who play by the rules, even when those on the outside—those who live by different rules—find ours unjust, incomprehensible, even repellent.

It follows, then, that self and society are inextricably interwoven, that the one does not exist without the other, that the customs, values, beliefs, and roles of any society are internalized so deeply by its citizens that they come to believe they are their own.

Witness, for example, the mothers and grandmothers in some African tribes who impose on their daughters the ritual female circumcision that not only brought them pain but left them crippled in both body and spirit. Some say the mothers do this to their daughters because they won't be marriageable otherwise, a virtual death sentence for a woman in these societies. No doubt that's true. But another truth is that the older women have so internalized those customs that they believe them to be right and just, the only way to live and be a woman. Which in turn makes it possible for the daughters to accept their mutilation, even desire it as the mark of their entry into the community of women and, what's more, to believe they're making a free choice.

So it is with old age in our society. The beliefs and attitudes about age that surround us inevitably color how we think of ourselves. When I was sixty and got stuck in my writing, no one ever said to me, as an acquaintance to whom I was complaining recently did, "Let's face it, you're past eighty and your brain's not so nimble anymore." He didn't think he was being cruel; he was just saying what he knows to be true. And indeed, it wasn't the first time I'd heard those words. I've been saying them to myself ever since I took on this project.

Is it any wonder that I take what sometimes seems to me to be inordinate pride in looking much younger than I am? Since I turned eighty two years ago, I tell whoever will listen how old I am because I want to hear them respond with wonder, with some version of, "No, you're kidding; I'd never have guessed." An observation that invariably pleases and shames me—pleases me because I love to hear those words, shames me for the same reason, because it has become so important to me not to look like *them*, even while I know I'm one of them.

So why do I continue to do it? No doubt the main reason is the obvious one: the pleasure outweighs the pain. But it's also a way of getting in their face, of saying, "Never mind what you've always believed; look at me, this is also eighty-two."

My puny efforts notwithstanding, there's no getting around the fact that if society is revolted by the aged, old people are revolted by themselves. I look at my naked body, at the flesh that hangs from my upper arms, the breasts that droop, the belly that bulges, and I experience a small shock, a shiver of disgust. I turn away, wanting to cover myself as quickly as possible, to clothe myself with garments bought in the hope they'll hide what I don't want the world to see. Once dressed, I look in the mirror and see a small, slim woman whose image leaves me relieved: *I can still fake it, cover it up.* What's the *it?* Being old, of course.

I worry about my arms and belly; Nora Ephron worries about her neck. "If anyone young is reading this, go right this minute, put on a bikini and don't take it off until you're thirty-four," she commands. After that it's downhill all the way. By the time you're forty-three, she announces, you'd better hide your neck. The creams, lotions, oils may help the face fake it, but the neck tells the tale. "Our faces are lies and our necks are the truth," she insists.[2] And true to her word, the photograph on the book jacket shows her well covered with a turtleneck up over her chin.

Medical advances, changing lifestyles, a new sense of what's possible if we take care of our bodies have made an enormous difference in pushing back the aging process. But we know when we're getting old, even when we don't want to know it. For however successfully we manage to cover up the visible signs of our aging, we don't fool our bodies. An hour a day on the StairMaster may increase our aerobic capacity, but the body continues to change in predictable ways. Memory slips, we get tired when we didn't before, various body parts don't work as well as they used to, aches and pains appear in places we didn't know we had. The doctor, when we see him, listens to our complaints, shakes his head, and says kindly, "Yes, things begin to wear out; it's all a natural part of the aging process."

So natural, in fact, that the experts can pretty much tell us when each of our five senses will begin its decline. Any single person may have a different experience, of course, but in general it goes like this: hearing begins to diminish in the mid-forties, vision and touch in the mid-fifties, taste in the late fifties, and smell in the mid-seventies.

What fifty-year-old hasn't experienced some of these changes? What sixty-five-year-old hasn't mourned the loss of sexual urgency, and with it the sense of manliness he thought was his birthright until then? What seventy-year-old hasn't looked at her body with an aching heart as she searched vainly for that smooth, slim young thing she used to know? What eighty-year-old doesn't know what it means to be tired in ways he never understood before?

If middle age is the time when the first real signs of physical change and decline appear, old age is the culmination of the process. Death, which was still a distant threat in the earlier years, is closer now. The lines time started to etch at midlife are more like furrows than wrinkles now, hair that was still half dark then is completely grayed, words more often refuse to come when we want them, memory continues to retreat until the distant past may seem closer than yesterday. We can erase the lines with surgery and Botox, cover the gray with dyes, practice memory aids assiduously, but there's no way to avoid the internal sense of loss and the sadness that accompanies old age—sorrow that's made exponentially worse by a culture that glorifies youth and sells it so unrelentingly.

If we consolidated our identity at midlife and thought the job was done, old age is when we lose it, when we have to rethink ourselves yet again, figure out who we are now that the roles and life tasks that consumed us and formed the center of our sense of self are finished. This, I believe, is one reason why those of us who are old spend so much time looking backward. "My yesterdays walk with me. They keep step, they are gray faces that peer over my shoulder," writes William Golding. And, I might add, they are also the faces that remind us who we once were. When we turn our gaze back, we live for a moment in the reflected glory of the past, hoping that others will notice and appreciate the whole of us, not just who they see in the present.

But the deeper motive for bringing the yesterdays into today, perhaps the one that's not fully conscious, is the need to re-vision ourselves, to bring all the selves we've known through our lifetime into a new and expanded self, a self that's more than just a collection of losses, one that can live more comfortably in what is almost inevitably an uncomfortable present.

Chapter Six

The Golden Years?
They've Gotta Be Kidding!

I was tired of working so hard, doing the same thing for so many years, so I retired a couple of years ago, figuring this was my chance at the golden years," says a seventy-two-year-old, his words etched in bitterness. "It was okay for a while, but all the 'fun' stuff doesn't seem like fun anymore, so now what? There's got to be something more than waking up wondering what the hell you're going to do with your day." He pauses, looks out the window at a view that would make anyone smile, turns pained eyes back to me, and snorts, "The golden years? They've gotta be kidding! If this is gold what's brass?"

In 1979 I published a book that included a chapter titled "What Am I Going to Do with the Rest of My Life?" Then, I was writing about women who, at forty, found themselves facing a frighteningly empty future. "Pretty much the whole of adult life was supposed to be around helping your husband and raising your children," exclaimed a forty-two-year-old woman who epitomized the dilemma of that era. "I mean, I never thought about what happens to the rest of life. Then all of a sudden, he doesn't need your help anymore and the children are raised. Now what?"[1]

Much has changed in the intervening decades. Then, most forty-year-old women had devoted themselves to being wife and mother only to awaken to the realization that they no longer knew who they were beyond the confines of those roles. Now, the same women have most likely been in the labor force for years and, as a result, have a broader, less elusive sense of self. Now, instead of bearing her first child at nineteen or twenty, a woman is likely to be twenty-six, and for a significant subsection of the population, much older, maybe even forty.

In the mid-twentieth century, when American life expectancy hovered around sixty-five, forty was on the cusp of middle age; questions about the "rest of life" presumed something like twenty more years, and it was mainly women who asked them. Men knew what the rest of their lives would bring. If they were lucky enough to live to retirement, they'd get a party, a gold watch, and not much time to enjoy it. Now a man who reaches the age of sixty-five can expect to live into his early eighties, a woman even later.[2]

It's not just the privileged middle class who can count on living so many extra years. For while class, race, and ethnicity play a part in determining life expectancy in our nation, and while those in the white middle- and upper-middle class are indeed the most privileged in this as well as other aspects of their lives, the inequalities in life span are smaller today than at any earlier moment in history.

As we live longer, healthier lives, the question "Now what?" comes later, for some at sixty, for others not until seventy or more. But no matter how delayed, the question will arise with the same inevitability that death itself arrives on our doorstep. It makes no difference what our station is, whether high or low, we will all stand at the abyss as, by the very nature of living so long, we are forced to look into a future we cannot know and confront the combination of hope and fear that accompanies that reality.

"I wouldn't know what else to do," said Mike Wallace, the renowned television journalist, when, at eighty-eight, he was asked when he might leave the show at which he'd worked since 1968. When, a short time later, he suddenly announced his retirement without explanation, his former producer, Don Hewitt, speaking from his own experience, explained, "You get to a certain age . . . and you're not as gung-ho as you thought you were going to be. But you hang onto *who you were* [italics added] because you don't know any better."[3] To *who you were*, not *what you do*, because, as is so often the case, what you do becomes who you are.

I can almost hear some voices arguing that this isn't necessarily true among working-class men and women for whom what they do is just a job, not the definition of self. While there may be a kernel of truth in that view, it's also the conceit of the professional class that people who aren't as well educated as they, people who work with their hands instead of their heads, can't possibly find work fulfilling, let alone self-defining.

But talk to working-class people, listen to what they say about themselves, and you hear a more complex story. Not surprisingly, women, even those who work outside the home, have a more fluid and multifaceted sense of their own identity than men—a fact, parenthetically, that's true about women of any class. So while they may value their work life, they still define themselves in various ways: wife, mother, worker, daughter, usually depending upon which claims the center of their attention at the time of the conversation, none necessarily taking precedence over the other.

For the men it's different. While working-class men generally may be less attached than professionals to the actual work they do, the fact that they have a job to which they go every day is the central identity-defining feature of their lives. In hundreds of interviews with working-class men over more than three decades, I never spoke with one, not even a man who found little satisfaction in the job itself, who didn't start a description of himself by telling me what kind of work he did. Not that he was a husband, son, father, not where he lived, what he cared about, or what hobbies he may have had, but what he did for a living. Work, whatever it was, whether they liked it or not, defined them, established their status as men who deserved attention and respect. I'm a "working man" they declared proudly, words meant to suggest they were *real* men, not like those "pencil pushers" who, according to many of them, "never did an honest day's work in their lives."[4]

This isn't to say working-class people are content with their lot, only that they find ways to compensate, to rework the common assumptions about the value of their place in this status-driven society in ways that enhance their self-regard and allow them some psychological ease.

Whatever the class or gender differences or similarities may be, one fact is indisputable: all of us are now in uncharted territory, a stage of life not seen before in human history. And whether woman or man, whether working-class or professional, we're all wondering how we'll live, what we'll do, who we'll be for the next twenty or thirty years.

For lack of a better alternative, many people remain on the job well beyond what was once the accepted retirement age. Some, generally professional women and men who find satisfaction in their work and whose identity is closely tied to it, do so out of choice.

"I love my job; I love to teach; I can't imagine giving it up," exclaims a seventy-six-year-old college professor. Then, with a rueful smile, "Well, I guess the day will come when it won't be my choice, won't it? I can't imagine life without it."

Many more stay in the work force or return to it after retirement out of need, sometimes economic, sometimes psychological, often a combination of both. The economic side is straightforward. In a nation driven by consumerism, where our president, seeking to restore public calm after September 11, advised his people to go out and shop, where 62 percent of people over fifty-five have less than $100,000 in savings[5] and the median value of retirement accounts for those between fifty-five and sixty-four is $88,000,[6] where economists who watch such things tell us that Americans are spending more than they earn, that household debt rose by 132 percent of disposable income in 2005,[7] and that debt payments consume close to 20 percent of the average family's income and much more for those on the lower rungs of the economic ladder[8]—only the very rich have enough savings and investments to support their lifestyle.

Most pensions, when they exist, aren't adequate to sustain the lifestyle people are accustomed to, many not even enough to meet basic needs, and, in any case, rarely keep pace with inflation. For those with no pension and limited savings, the choice is scrimping or going back to work; those who managed to put aside a nest egg are forced to deplete it.

"I did everything I was supposed to do, even managed to save a fair amount of money for retirement," says an eighty-four-year-old who retired nearly twenty years ago, went back into the work force eight years later, and recently retired again. "But the pension wasn't enough, and it seemed like the savings were gone in a blink. Who knew I'd still be alive so many years after I gave up working?"

Psychologically, it's more complicated. While their middle-aged children dream of a life beyond the rat race, one-third of their "retired" parents are back in the work force, and two-thirds of those say they're there at least as much out of desire as economic need. During their working years, they looked forward to retirement with fantasies about all the things they couldn't do when they were working, whether going fishing, playing golf, re-modeling the kitchen, or spending more time with the grand-children. Then reality hit.

From the attorney to the truck driver, from the homemaker to the executive, the complaints are the same. Without work, without something to structure their days, something that marks the difference between Sunday and Monday, something that sig-nals that they still have a place in the world, life is stripped of much of its meaning.

"Okay, so I pick my grandchildren up from school two days a week, and I love the time we have together. But what about the rest of the time?" asks a seventy-four-year-old retired social worker. "Sure, I keep busy, but that's just what it is—keeping busy. It doesn't have a lot of meaning, if you know what I mean."

The pleasures they'd looked forward to are indeed pleasura-ble, but not quite enough to still the restlessness that sets in—the sense that there must be something more—or to quiet the inter-nal voice that asks so insistently: *Now what?*

"I used to think life would be perfect if I could play golf every day," remarks a seventy-six-year-old former salesman. "What can I tell you? Now I know that even if I did, there'd still be too many days in the week. I mean, I love it but . . ." His words trail off, as if searching for a way to avoid the thought he doesn't want to speak.

"But what?" I coach.

A deep sigh. "I don't know what to say; it's just not enough. It's not a life, that's all."

Go to any mall in America that houses stores like Home De-pot, Wal-Mart, Target, Costco, and all the other retail outlets that eagerly hire older workers, and you'll see formerly retired women and men on the floor, usually doing jobs well below their capacity. It's a good deal for the companies. Older workers, un-like their baby boomer children, have little sense of entitlement.

They don't complain, don't ask for anything, and are more reliable than younger workers. If that isn't enough to soothe any manager's anxious heart, retirees are happy to work part-time, which means they don't qualify for benefits—a big boost to the company's bottom line.

It sounds like exploitation, and it is. But in this case, what's good for business also works for those in need, who have few or no options. And indeed there are few for the older people who looked forward to retirement, thought it would be a walk on the sunny side, only to find themselves on a cold and lonely path. Even if they wanted to, they can't go back to the job they left, and they're not likely to find another one like it. So they take what they can get.

"I retired a couple of years ago because I thought it was time to stop working and start living," says a seventy-year-old former forklift operator. "But after a couple of years, it got pretty damn old. My wife got tired of me moping around the house with nothing to do. I mean, how often can you tune up the car or fix the damn stopped drain? I just couldn't take it anymore. I woke up one morning and thought, Christ, if this is life, what's being dead like? Don't get me wrong, I don't love this job I've got now, but at least I'm back out in the world, and that's a lot better than sitting around the house drinking beer and wondering what I'm going to do today." Then he added, with a wry smile, "The extra cash doesn't hurt either."

It's a story I heard repeatedly in one version or another, including during a recent appearance on a local radio talk show. We weren't five minutes into a discussion about retirement and what it means today before the phone lines were jammed with women and men wanting to speak their experience about the difficulty of finding meaning in a life so drastically different from what they'd known.

When I left the studio, the security guard who had escorted

me in was waiting to lead me out. She had seemed, when we met an hour earlier, to be a quiet, deferential woman I judged to be in her late sixties. When she met me after the show, I hardly recognized her as the same person. She was ebullient, a huge smile lighting up her face, words pouring out uncontained and unfiltered.

"Go, girl; right on," she exulted, practically dancing with joy. "Everything you said is right. Did you hear all those people talking to you; they know you're right, too. It's why I work here. I worked all my life since I was thirteen years old, cleaning houses, raising my kids, doing all kinds of lousy jobs until I finally worked myself up to a nurse's aide at The General [local slang for San Francisco's County Hospital]. Hard work that is, sad, too, people sick and dying and needing and sometimes nobody there for them.

"I used to think, boy, I'm going to be glad to get out of here. My husband, he left me a little insurance money and a pension when he died last year, and I thought, yeah, it's time to take it easy. So I retired, thinking I was going to have me a good time. But it didn't work out that way."

"Why?" I asked. "Wasn't there enough money?"

She laughed, "Well, you know, a little more money never hurt, but no, that's not the real reason why I'm here. I just couldn't stand being retired. I mean, the days dragged by, and I felt useless. I tell my kids, you better think about what you're going to do when you get finished working, because you can't figure on dying these days. But those young people, they don't believe it; they think it'll all come up roses. Just wait, they'll see."

Then, as she saw me out the door, she leaned toward me and said more quietly, "Girl, you keep on keeping on. You're doing good; people need to know they're not the only ones feeling what they're feeling."

I climbed into my car and drove home, so preoccupied with

the tape in my head that kept rerunning everything I'd heard that morning that I missed my freeway exit.

A colleague, reading these words in a draft version of this chapter, asked: "What about women like my mother, who's in her late eighties and never worked outside the home? Her life doesn't seem all that different than when she was middle-aged, and maybe not even when she was raising us."

I think about her words, think about the women I met in the course of writing this book—those who had worked outside the home and those who had not—who spoke without prompting about the difficulty of living a life without a meaningful social role, one that affirms their presence in the world and validates their importance in it.

"The hardest thing about this time of life is feeling useless," explains a seventy-two-year-old woman who never held a paid job. "I used to feel like there was a purpose to my life, but now with my husband gone and my children... What can I say, nobody needs me anymore."

How, I wonder, could it be otherwise, in a society that values usefulness above all else?

Whether in the public world of work or in the private world of family, the loss of the roles that ground us, that define us to ourselves and to the social world in which we live, is rarely if ever met with ease and equanimity. Why, then, would we assume that men suffer when they lose the role that centered their lives, and women don't, that men need to feel useful and productive, but not women?

True, their experience is different, tinged as it is by the gendered roles of the past, by who they were and what they did then, by the fact that it was generally the family roles that defined women, while for men it was largely their place in the world of work. But none of this changes the fact that for those women who never worked outside the home, being mother and housewife *was* the job, and they feel the loss as keenly as any man who's paid for his work.

Where, then, did the idea of "the golden years" come from? Is this just media hype that has no relation to the reality of people's experience in old age? Or was it a more or less apt description of some earlier time? Maybe when people lived only a few years after retirement, the relief from a lifetime of work and tight schedules, the freedom to allow themselves to expand fully into the space they inhabit, to take up activities they never had time for before, did indeed make those years golden. Maybe so many of us feel them so differently now because they last so long.

I think about my mother, who retired from her factory job in New York's garment industry when she was sixty-five years old. Those first few years were wonderful. She traveled, saw the world beyond the borders of New York City for the first time in her adult life, visited her children and grandchildren, none of whom lived nearby, and agreed to let me hire a tutor to teach her to read and write so she could be relieved of the stigma of illiteracy that had shamed her throughout her life.

I don't know whether she would have called those years golden, but she certainly seemed more at peace than I'd ever seen her. But the years kept piling on, and pretty soon she was seventy, then eighty and still counting, until finally, all she could say when I came to visit was: "Why doesn't God take me? Who needs to live so long?"

She wasn't ill or infirm; that wouldn't happen until shortly before she died at ninety-four. But after a while, she couldn't, maybe didn't want to, sustain the renewed vigor with which she had approached life immediately after her retirement. If there were opportunities still waiting, she couldn't see them. It was as if she had lived her life and was finished; anything more was burdensome.

Such feelings are not unknown to many of us at this stage of life. Indeed, for most of us, even those who are healthy and active, our extended old age will most likely feel like some combination of a blessing and a curse. Certainly there are moments when we enjoy what feels like the "warm autumn" celebrated in a *New York Times Magazine* article titled, "The Age Boom."[9] There's something to be said for being freed of responsibility, for waking up each day to the knowledge that you're not obliged to perform, for having the time to read the novels you've hungered for but couldn't get to before, for feeling you've earned the right to pick and choose what you'll do, when you'll do it, and with whom you'll do it.

"Maybe the one good thing I can say about getting old is that I'm more likely than ever before to do what I want and say what I feel," explains a seventy-five-year-old professional woman who's still working part-time. "Before, I was always worried about what other people would think; now I don't care in the same way. So if someone wants me to do something I really don't want to do, I'll say no. I just don't put up with what I used to accept before.

"I had lunch with a friend recently, someone I've known for many years but don't have that much of a connection with anymore. She complained that she doesn't see enough of me, and I was able to say what I could never have said before: 'I'm sorry, but this is what it is; it's as much as I can give.'"

But these newfound freedoms come with a price. Ask anyone who is living this new life stage and you'll hear also about the times when it feels like a cold winter. For along with the gift of time comes the realization that time itself is now finite, that we hold the end always in our sights. It's a showstopper. A fifty-four-year-old friend tells me he'd like us to join him and his family on a trip next year, and all I can think is: *If we're still here then.*

How do you plan for a future when you don't know when time will stop? That's true for all of us, of course, but for the old it has an immediacy that can't be denied. It's not just the realization that we're close to the end that makes this time so difficult. For the pleasure in our freedom to "just be" comes with the understanding that it's possible only because we've become superfluous, because we've lost our place in the world, because our presence is no longer needed, and that in addition to being unnecessary—or perhaps because of it—we've also become invisible, just another one of the old people, featureless and indistinguishable from one another, who take up space on the bus.

"No memory of having starred / Atones for later disregard, / Or keeps the end from being hard," writes Robert Frost. I read the words and think: *Disregard, yes, but it's also more than that.* It's being invisible, being seen only as part of the group, not as an individual. "You know what I miss as I get older?" asked Mary Cantwell in a conversation with novelist Jean Rhys. "That look of anticipation in a man's eyes when he first meets you."

"Yes," sighed Ms. Rhys, then well over eighty and not far from death, "I miss it still."[10]

It's a painful reality for older women, one that highlights the historic gender differences. Men, even those who age badly, usually have no trouble finding companionship, sexual and otherwise. It's a common tale, so well known and observed it needs no documentation: men who are old, fat, and bald marry attractive, slender women twenty or more years their junior as if it's their birthright.

"Scarcity," says a male friend to whom I make this observation. "It's a market phenomenon, a matter of scarce resources." True, women outlive men by a very large margin,[11] but scarcity alone doesn't explain the differences in the social-sexual desirability of women and men. Rather it's a matter of value and social power, and even in old age, men retain both in ways women never had them.

A 2006 film, *The Boynton Beach Club*, about a community

of retirees, gives testimony to the truth of this observation. A woman whose husband dies is befriended by another woman; no man in sight. A man who loses his wife has a freezer full of casseroles delivered by women eager to show off their wares, while all he wants is a quiet space to grieve. Until, that is, a svelte blonde comes along to entice him with something besides food. Scenes that made my feminist soul squirm with discomfort while I also knew they spoke the truth.

Still, outside the social-sexual arena, even men aren't immune to the invisibility of age, which follows all of us into many corners of life where we used to be seen, whether on the job or in the social world. How can it be otherwise in a society that idolizes youth, that has little reverence for its own history, that moves so quickly that yesterday's knowledge is rendered obsolete today? In such a social setting, whatever wisdom about life we who are old have gathered seems like ancient history, not . . . What's that word that has been so prominent in our national discourse for the last several decades? Ah yes, "relevance." We're not relevant.

"I'm a lot smarter today than I was thirty years ago, and I'm better at my job now than I was then," says a sixty-five-year-old executive who lost his job to one of those corporate mergers we know so well these days. "But these yo-yo kids who are in charge don't even see me and what I can do; they only see my age, and that's the end of it."

A plight common enough to warrant a *New Yorker* cartoon featuring a cigar-smoking, bewildered-looking seventy-something man looking out the window of the office he's about to leave for good and saying ruefully, "I think I've acquired some wisdom over the years, but there doesn't seem to be much demand for it."

In a nation that puts such a high premium on work and productivity, where personal identity is defined primarily by what we do for a living, not being "in demand" is a hard place to be. It's almost as if we don't exist. Think about it: How do you place someone on first meeting? What's the first question asked of you after the introductions are made? What's the first thing *you* ask?

"What do you do?" Until you have the answer, the person before you is virtually a cipher, a form without much content. When we know what job she holds, we can fill in the shape, place her in the class, status, and social hierarchy that lives in our mind, even when we don't consciously think in those terms. It tells us what the common ground might be, gives us a start, some basis for beginning a conversation with a stranger. Or, as is sometimes the case, it warns us off.

"One of the first questions on meeting you is, 'What do you do?' and I no longer know how to answer that question," writes some unnamed blogger I found on the Web. "It may be vanity or prejudice based on faulty, past perception, but 'I'm retired' is not a phrase that will pass my lips any time soon."[12]

It isn't vanity or misperception. He avoids the word, as so many retirees do, because to use it makes him feel vulnerable, as if he has no place in the world, no self to present to it. Pulitzer Prize winner Robert Butler,[13] the founding director of the National Institute of Aging, speaks about the cost of being identified as retired and his own resistance to using what he calls "the R word."

> When I stepped down as the chair of geriatrics at Mount Sinai to build the Longevity Center, people began to refer to me as "retired." I quickly realized that "retired" was not a good word. If you are applying for grants from the N.I.H., you don't want to be perceived as "retired," which seems to be a synonym for "over the hill."[14]

If Robert Butler, a man who almost single-handedly created the field of aging and its serious study, who at eighty still heads up the International Longevity Center, a research and policy organization affiliated with Mount Sinai School of Medicine in New York City, feels the chill of "the R word," what chance do ordinary men and women have?

"I didn't used to mind it when the first thing people I didn't know asked was, 'What do you do?' " remarks a retired sixty-nine-year-old former executive. "Now I hate it; I hate having nothing to say. If I say I'm retired," he continues, shaking his head as if to wipe out the image of the word, "it's like saying I'm nothing, and it's not just in my head. I see how people react when I say it; it's like they don't know what to say after that. Then, finally, they say something dumb, like 'Hey, that's great,' and go talk to someone else."

Hmmm! That's exactly what women used to complain about when they had to answer "housewife" to the what-do-you-do question, a designation that was upgraded to "homemaker" but that made little difference in how quickly the questioner turned away. "It's payback time," I think with a moment of malicious pleasure as I wonder how many times this man did that to some woman.

The scars I bear from the years when I was made to feel like "nothing" because all I could say was "housewife" have faded, but the memory of being written off with barely another word can still bring a chill and a shot of anger at the way we—women, old people, whoever—feel forced to deny ourselves in order to be seen, feel impelled to make up an answer to the what-do-you-do question to keep people from walking away.

I can't get the word "retired" out of my mouth today any more comfortably than I was able to say "housewife" all those many years ago. Nor can my ninety-year-old husband do anything but shift and dodge when he's asked the question, and finally quip, "A writer never retires." It's not true, of course, but it saves him from the need to confront publicly the truth that he has been retired—meaning, in social terms, "nobody"—for years now.

I'm keenly aware, too, that, for the first time since I laid my-self off as a writer a few years ago, it's enormously relieving to be able to claim a recognized public self again, to say once more "I'm a writer"—present tense not past—instead of fumbling around explaining how I'm becoming an artist. Indeed, it's probably one of the reasons why I accepted the invitation to write this book. For the moment, at least, I'm freed from the delicate balancing act of sustaining a sense of self without a valued social identity.

I can almost hear some readers say: Wait a minute; it can't be that grim. My Aunt Sally is retired, and she doesn't seem to be troubled by the word or the idea. My Uncle Joey moved into one of those retirement communities a couple of years ago and loves it.

Yes, there certainly are plenty of Aunt Sallys and Uncle Joeys who find some pleasure and comfort in these years, just as many of the people who complain the loudest will grant that there are times when their lives look pretty good to them. But no matter which side someone falls on, it's almost never cleanly unambiva-lent, rarely without some deeply felt understanding of the diffi-culties of these years, whether physically, emotionally, or both, seldom without the knowledge that they don't count in the world in the way they did before they retired.

True, there have been more media stories than I can count about the wonders of the retirement communities—or "active adult communities" as they have recently been renamed—about the endless round of activities they offer, about the classes, and the dances, and the parties, and the shows. I've visited some of these communities, talked to people who live in them, listened to them tell me how much they love living there, how much fun it is, how they're so busy all the time that they have little time for anything else. "We're more social here than we've ever been before," says one woman. "I just turned seventy and do hula danc-ing," exults another, whose husband is taking tap-dancing lessons. "We're so busy all the time; it's like a whirlwind, no time to think about anything," explains a third.

But tell me, am I the only one who looks at this level of frantic activity and wonders what's going on behind it? I don't mean to dismiss the experience of others in favor of psychological interpretations, but I can't help asking: How much of the "fun" is a race against time? How much is a denial of their fear of facing their mortality? How much is pure escape from the realities they'd have to face if they slowed down to contemplate them? Nothing wrong with any of that, but these surely are questions worth asking.

My questions notwithstanding, I also believe that, given the indignities of aging in this society, retirement communities serve an important function for those who choose to live in them. They move from a world where they no longer have a place, a world where age is stigma, to one where they are celebrated. Who wouldn't like that? They go from the world where the cocktail party question du jour is, "What do you do?" to a place where no one is supposed to ask or care, where people make great effort to accept one another for who they are today, not who or what they might have been yesterday. Who wouldn't feel good there?

But here's the caveat. Look around these communities, talk with people in them, and you see a much more complicated picture than the chirpy, good-news-about-aging the media tales present—or even what their relatives want to believe. Uncle Joey might tell his nephew that he's having a great time, and in some ways he is. But when someone who knows what old age is all about comes along and really wants to hear his story, it's toned with shades of gray, not black or white.

Moreover, it's often the new residents and largely those we might call the young old—those between about sixty-two (usually the bottom age at which people can enter) and seventy-four —who are having such a good time. And not even all of these.

As one manager explained, "There's the go-go folks, the go-slow people, and the no-go ones." But even for those who start out as go-go's, by the time they've been there a few years, the activities begin to pale into more of the same, and the sense that there must be more to life than this begins to take hold.

"We moved in here eleven years ago, and I thought it was great," explains a seventy-seven-year-old man. "But now..." He's silent for a moment, his eyes roaming the room, then, "Look, don't misunderstand, I still think it's a great place to live at this age, but..." Another pause, then, "Well, that's the point, isn't it—*at this age* [emphasis his]." He shakes his head sadly as he thinks about what he's just said. "It's like been there, done that, so then you begin to ask, what's left?"

For those who live outside such communities, it's pretty much the same. The early retirement years may be pleasurable, may even be wonderful for some. But as the years pass, many begin to complain that they're living too long, that life no longer has meaning.

"What's the point. I can't do all the things I used to do any-more, and I don't even want to," exclaims an eighty-nine-year-old woman. "What? Another trip to someplace I've already been to too many times? Another club meeting? I know before I get there what everyone in my book club is going to say. I'm tired; it's time to lay my head down and go. What are those scientists do-ing, using all that brain power to get us to live longer? I want to know, what's the point?"

What's the point? It's not a frivolous question. I ask a mid-sixties friend if she'd like to live to one hundred, and she replies with a grimace, a shudder, and an unequivocal "No."

"Why?" I want to know.

"What would I do for all those years?" she asks.

A reply I got from many of the people I met of whom I asked the same question. There's some ambivalence, of course. How could there not be? We're talking about *death*—the ultimate finality. But bottom line, most people offer a resounding no to the question, as does Frank Bruni, the food critic at the *New York Times*, in his droll and poignant column on the subject.

> If living to 99 means forever cutting the porterhouse into eighths, swearing off the baked potato and putting the martini shaker in storage, then 85 sounds a whole lot better, and I'd ratchet that down to 79 to hold onto the Haagen-Dazs, along with a few shreds of spontaneity. It's a matter of priorities.
>
> Do we really want as many years as we can get, no matter how we get them? At what point does the pursuit of an extended life ... become the entire business of life? Is longevity all it's cracked up to be? ... Each of us can individually hunker down for the long haul ... exercising faithfully so that our limbs stay as limber as our nipped-and-tucked faces are taut. But doesn't the quality of our days matter as much as the quantity of them?[15]

To which I and many others say, "Amen!"

Chapter Seven

... And Now About Sex

Geezer sex, once a bad joke, an idea that made us squirm uncomfortably—*old people doing it!*—is now the topic of the day, with ads featuring older people looking soulfully into each other's eyes as they make their way to the nearest bed. Of course, the people in the ads never *look* like any old person we know. Sure, there's a line here, a brow that isn't perfectly smooth, a little gray at the temples, just enough so we'll know they're supposed to be like us. But they're always tall, slim, fit, and handsome, no bags or sags or drooping bellies, no cares or canes, just the wonderful anticipation of sexual joy.

We're surrounded with sexual imagery, reminded of what we must be missing if we're not living in some kind of inspired sexual ecstasy. Magazines, newspapers, and the Web publish hundreds, if not thousands, of articles about sex each month, while films show aging stars like Jack Nicholson and Diane Keaton happily getting it on.[1] Bookstore shelves are lined with uncounted numbers of volumes ranging from scholarly treatises to breezy self-help books that advise us of the need to be inventive if we're to keep the sexual fires burning, instruct us on what to do and how to do it, assure us that anything goes so long as it's consensual, and promise a lifetime of sexual pleasure if we only follow the rules. And just in case we're not already anxious enough, they provide self-tests so we can judge how we're doing.

For those of us who long ago left the hot sexual fires of youth behind, there are special messages and advice on how to recapture that time. Not that anyone asks whether that's something we want. Sure, some women would like to feel more sexually vigorous, and some men may yearn for the time when they walked around in a near-perpetual state of sexual readiness. But even they will likely agree that, as one sixty-eight-year-old man remarked, "We knew how to screw; we didn't know what the real thing was then. For that you have to grow up."

Or as a divorced sixty-two-year-old male friend, reflecting on Gail Sheehy's *Sex and the Seasoned Woman*,[2] writes: "I don't know about those women Sheehy writes about who are so hot to trot. I think anyone past fifty learned long ago that hot sex doesn't last as long as a good conversation, and that's what I want now before I go to bed with a woman. So if they're really out there, they better brush up on their social skills. The other stuff may come later, or it may not, but it's sure not the first thing on the plate for me and a lot of other guys."

Plug "sex in old age" into Google, and, depending on the day, you'll come up with somewhere around 40 million hits; change the search word to "Viagra" and it returns a whopping 60+ million, many of them extolling the wonders of sex in old age—now delicately labeled "mature sex"—along with thousands of ads offering pills that promise a "rock hard erection" that will put "man" back into manly. But buyer beware: call your doctor at once if that erection lasts for more than four hours.

There's no pill yet for women, but not to worry. There's a plastic surgeon around the corner who will be happy to rejuvenate the vagina and make it as tight and pink and welcoming as—yes, that's right—when we were young.

"Can you imagine having surgery to tighten your vagina?"

gasped a seventy-six-year-old woman I spoke with. "I saw it on that TV program about plastic surgeons who do things like that. I think we must be going crazy."

Commenting on the Viagra phenomenon, Dr. Abraham Morgentaler, a practicing urologist and member of the Harvard Medical School faculty, writes about the fantasies Viagra let loose and how detached they are from the complexity of human sexuality.

> Viagra quickly tapped into a set of wishful fantasies that mirrored our culture's hunger for certainty and a quick fix. Supported by stories that described elderly men restored to such sexual vitality by Viagra that they abandoned their wives in favor of younger women, a conventional wisdom arose that Viagra was a fountain of youth, a sure cure, the real deal. Baby boomers could now look forward to fabulous sex well into their nineties. . . . But there is clearly more to the story of human sexuality and relationships than the Viagra Myth would have us believe.[3]

Or to paraphrase a famous Clinton-era slogan: "It's the relationship, stupid!" A lesson the old learned long ago as they look on in wonder: *Who can they possibly be talking about?* Remember when it used to be fun? we say to each other. Remember when we didn't have to think about it, plan for it, work so hard at it? we ask each other, while wondering silently if something is wrong with us because, while others are allegedly aching for sex, we're mostly content with a hug and a cuddle.

I read the media tales about the rollicking sex in nursing homes and wonder where they come from. This isn't to say that no one in a nursing home ever has sexual intercourse, or that men and women of any age don't yearn for intimate touch and reach out for it when they can. But swinging sex? I don't think so.

What I hear most often from older people whose partner is

no longer with them is not that they miss sex itself, but that they feel deprived of the physical closeness, of not experiencing the other's touch anymore.

"I used to think I missed sex and, I don't know, I guess I did; I mean, after all, it's a big thing to lose," says a seventy-eight-year-old man who's still mourning his wife's death two years earlier and whose own health is fragile. "It's maybe the hardest thing about getting old, not being able to perform so well anymore—or maybe not at all. But now that she's gone, all I really miss is her body next to mine; the bed's empty. I miss being able to reach out and touch her and, you know, being touched by her. I never knew how important that part was until I didn't have it anymore. I just miss having somebody to hold."

How is it that the people who write a different story about sex and aging don't talk to the same people I do? The sixty-nine-year-old woman who says, "I have to say I don't miss sex at all and feel relieved not to have to do it, although occasionally I do fantasize about the past and future—but not enough to call it missing." Or the seventy-four-year-old man whose prostate cancer left him impotent and who confesses, "It's funny. My body doesn't feel bad about not being able to do it, it's all up here," he says, pointing to his head. "I guess you could say it's sort of a relief in some way not to have to worry about performing anymore."

Where do they find the seventy-five-year-old men who, secure in the knowledge that the plumbing will always work, can't wait to jump into the sack? Or the women who, they tell us, blossom sexually in midlife and continue to flower through old age? Why do they feature stories about the seventy-something woman who advertises on an Internet dating site that she's seeking partners with whom to explore her sexuality, as if she were typical? Not that such women don't exist. They do, and I can add to those tales: women who come into their own in their later years, who never knew sexual fire in their youth and find it lit in their middle years. But seventy-five-year-old women yearning for sex? Well, maybe, but I've never met one, certainly not one who's living in a long-term marriage.

I realize, as I write these words, that others can ask the same question: Why don't *I* talk to the same people *they* do? The answer is: I do. But after more than three decades of interviewing people about sex, I know how hard it is for them to speak honestly about their sex lives, how likely they are to put a glossy finish on the story because it's a better fit with cultural expectations—and perhaps with the expectations of the interviewer—than their own experience. Who, in a nation that glorifies sex as the ultimate high, that has ratcheted up sexual expectations far beyond anything that's reasonably sustainable, wants to be the one to talk about sexual disenchantment or disinterest?

My experience, therefore, is that if you take the time to probe beneath the surface, even the good-news stories get far more complicated than the media representations. And what's more, there aren't many of them. So while tales of sexual athleticism at eighty may make younger people feel better when they contemplate their own future, I don't think it's wise to let the few speak for the many. Such distortion of what's real in the world, of what people can expect as they age, leads to the kind of confusion, disappointment, and self-doubt so many aging people experience. It's corrosive in any arena of living, but worse so in sex because it's the one thing, even more than money, that most people are reluctant to talk about.

Researchers into marriage and family life long ago discovered that each member of a family writes its biography differently and that husbands and wives often have what one prominent sociologist long ago labeled "his and her marriage"[4]—one marriage, two different stories to tell. Nowhere is this truer than in the sexual arena, and nowhere is that reality portrayed more eloquently than in the 1977 film *Annie Hall*, with Woody Allen playing a character named Alvy and Diane Keaton playing his longtime, live-in partner, Annie. In this memorable scene, they're each in their therapist's office, each bringing to the session their complaints about the other, while we, the audience, watch the action in both places on a split screen.

Alvy's therapist: "How often do you sleep together?" Alvy, lamenting: "Hardly ever. Maybe three times a week."

Annie's therapist: "Do you have sex often?" Annie, annoyed: "Constantly. I'd say three times a week."

Alvy and Annie were probably around forty, but adding years doesn't seem to do much to change the script, since I heard the same dissonance about sex between husbands and wives in this study. Among the older people, however, it's complicated by within-group differences, since sexual activity, especially intercourse, generally drops off in each decade from sixty-five through the nineties. While the heat of passion may be waning, the young old, those closer to sixty-five than seventy-five, are the most likely to continue to engage in a variety of sexual behaviors. After seventy-five, it slips a little more each year until the eighties, when it's generally all over but for the memories.

But no matter what the age, when I spoke with both partners in a marriage, there were likely to be distinct differences in the way they described their sexual experience, sometimes sounding as if they weren't in the same bed at the same time.

"I don't know about sex," demurs a sixty-nine-year-old woman, leaving me puzzled and waiting for the words to follow. "I mean, I sometimes think it's a lot more trouble than it's worth. My husband's having trouble, you know, I mean, he wants to but then he can't, and he feels terrible. I try to help him, you know, doing things that used to turn him on; sometimes it works and a lot of times it doesn't. So now, I'd be just as happy not to bother anymore, and even though he complains a lot, he feels the same way. It's like it's too much work."

A week or so later, I meet her seventy-four-year-old husband, who has quite another story.

"My wife, she always has her own version of events and sticks with them, no matter what. She says the problem is my ED [erectile dysfunction], but the truth is she's never been much one for sex and so, sure, you get older and it's not so urgent anymore, and you're tired of the fight, so you just let it go most of the time. And you know the saying, use it or lose it. Well, it's true."

He's thoughtful for a few moments, then adds, "It would be a lot different if she could work up some enthusiasm. But she's so damn negative about it all, it's like a deep freeze. I don't have trouble with it other times, I mean, when I see some bimbo strutting down the street, or when some of her friends come on to me at a party. The plumbing still works, just not with her," he concludes angrily, leaving me to wonder at what point he'll decide to take up one of those invitations and test himself out.

It's well understood and documented by acres of research that the urgency and intensity of sexual desire wanes in the context of a long-term marriage. Philosophy professor Edmund Leites, writing about marriage among the Puritans in seventeenth-century England, notes that "the price of constancy, fidelity, and steadiness of feeling is the sacrifice of intense excitement, at least in the sexual arena and perhaps in others as well."[5]

The reasons, I think, are subtle, not easily teased out. Certainly there's something about familiarity that acts as a brake on sexual desire in marriage. The excitement of anticipation is gone; we know what to expect, what he'll do, what she'll do, what it will take to consummate the act where both are sexually satisfied. It's why all sex manuals emphasize changing the routine, although they rarely understand how hard it is to do, how much habit and ritual and expectation frame our lives, how they die hard, whether in sex or in any other arena of living.

In his famous *Three Essays on Sexuality,* Freud writes about the importance of the unfamiliar, of obstacles to overcome, in heightening sexual desire.

It can easily be shown that the psychical value of erotic needs is reduced as soon as their satisfaction becomes easy. An obstacle is required in order to heighten libido; and where natural resistances to satisfaction have not been sufficient, men have at all times erected conventional ones so as to be able to enjoy love.[6]

Critics complain that Freud was writing about men and that he never understood women's sexuality. And I agree, but then, I'm not sure who fully understands what women's sexuality is really about. We have a whole feminist literature telling us that once released from its cultural chains women's sexual desire is at least as demanding and powerful as men's. As an abstract statement it may well be true, but sexual satisfaction doesn't live in the abstract. I don't mean to suggest that women don't have powerful spontaneous sexual urges, desires they can satisfy by themselves if they choose to, although most of the women in this study showed markedly little interest in masturbation.[7] But what makes a sexual *relationship* work for a woman, what makes her eager to climb into bed with a partner, generally has much more to do with relatedness than the simple satisfaction of a sexual urge.

That said, it's also true that few people who have lived in a marriage for any length of time would argue with Freud's thoughts on the subject.

"The problem is that there's no closed 'paren,' nothing brackets the experience of marriage," explains a sixty-five-year-old man speaking of his dissatisfaction with sex in his marriage.

"Maybe the terrible thing about married life is that it's endless, which gives you a whole different sense of time and possibilities. In a relationship that's not 'till death do us part,' you have to make each evening count or else there won't be another one, but when you're married, it's just another day, another night. Where's the excitement in that?"

His wife, who is both less eloquent and less interested in the subject, says simply, "It's okay with me if we never do it again. I don't know what else to say except that after a while, it just gets boring. And I'm not the only one who thinks so; it's what I hear from my friends, too."

For single people, it's a different story. For them, no matter what the age or experience, no matter how liberated a person may be, sex in the single life represents not just challenge but the mystery of the unknown, the uncharted, the illicit. Each new sexual encounter holds some danger, some test of self, some fear of the vulnerability the sex act inevitably evokes. All these are powerful aphrodisiacs; all generate feelings that stimulate and excite.

"Before you're married, it's like an audition," remarks a sixty-year-old woman who had been single for five years before she remarried a year ago. "Each time you're together it's like you're on trial. Even with lots of sexual experience, you feel unsure about things, you know: Will this be the one? Will it work? Is it right? And the older you get, the harder it is to think about taking off your clothes in front of somebody you hardly know. I think all that makes people cling to each other sexually so that bells ring and sparks fly. But," she concludes with a heavy sigh, "When I got married this time, I was too old to believe the sparks could last, and the truth is, they didn't."

It's not just the unfamiliar, then, not just the need to overcome obstacles, but the anxiety they create that is an important stimulator of sexual desire. It's a link that's rarely explored because we generally think of anxiety as inhibiting rather than inciting sexual appetite. And in certain circumstances it does just that—but not always, not even most of the time.

Ask people about their sexual experience when divorce comes into the picture, for example, and more often than not, they report that they had the best sex in years when they knew they were on the verge of parting—an experience that often leaves them perplexed and wondering if they're making the right decision. But change the viewing prism, and we can see that the renewed sexual excitement is at least in part because the relationship that once seemed without boundaries has become bracketed. It has an end, a realization that immediately raises some uncertainty about when, how, even if, which in turn creates anxiety that calls for something, some action that will hold the feelings at bay.

Some people go on shopping sprees: men buy new cars, women fill their already overstuffed closets with new clothes. And some ward anxiety off by an internal psychological process that transforms it into sexual need, which lends the encounter a level of excitement and intensity that had been long gone from the marriage bed.

Sex—what it means, how men and women experience the loss of their younger, more vibrant sexual selves—this is the one place in the drama of aging where the gender differences remain profound.[8] At the most obvious level, while the power dynamics inside marriage may have shifted in favor of wives as husbands become more dependent, in single life, they're more entrenched in male privilege than ever before. Again, it makes no difference how old a man is, what he looks like, what he does (or did) for a living, how much money he has, or even whether he has a hard time staying erect enough to have intercourse, there will almost always be a younger woman available if he wants one. But take even a casual look around the world of single women over sixty, and you'll see millions of very attractive women with no serious takers.

At a deeper, internal level, men and women experience the loss of sexual activity and desire quite differently as well. For women, who rarely if ever define themselves by their sexual prowess or conquests, sex for its own sake has little or no meaning; it's the loss of relatedness that's so hard.

"I miss sex," says a seventy-two-year-old friend, divorced and without a partner for ten years. When I remind her that she's turned down several opportunities in these years, she replies, "I'm not talking about sex for its own sake; I'm talking about a relationship, about being with someone I care about and who cares about me. Sex as a part of that, that's what I miss."

But for men whose sexual capacity and performance defines the very core of their manhood, sex is a major loss, no matter what their age.

"I haven't had an erection in years," says a ninety-year-old man, "but I still miss it and think about it. I look at an attractive woman and feel sorry I can't do anything about it."

"What is it you regret?" I ask.

He heaves a sigh and says, "What can I say? It's a big part of what being a man was all about."

When vaginal dryness, atrophy, or any of the other problems occur that lead to a woman giving up intercourse, she may feel the loss but it isn't an assault on her femininity. But for a man who gives up sex after too many failed attempts, it's a threat to the core of his masculinity. True, there may also be some relief in abandoning the struggle, but it's relief muddied by shame and humiliation, so humiliating that one man equated the loss with becoming like a woman.

"I might as well sit down to take a piss," says an eighty-year-old man, by way of explaining what it means to feel his sexual powers so diminished. "I don't mean any disrespect to you, but, you know, men stand up to piss; women sit down. That's the way it is. It's not even that I want to do it so much anymore; I mean, I think about it, but..." He shrugs, slipping into silence for a moment or two, then, "I don't know; I don't know what to say, except you don't feel like a real man when you can't get it up anymore."

Like everything else about growing old, the loss of sexual activity and desire doesn't happen all at once; it just gets harder and harder to keep working at it, and after a while, it slips away. Sometimes it's just the years that take their toll, sometimes it's the stress in the relationship, and not infrequently it's illness, physical or mental.

"It was a struggle for a few years," recalls an eighty-year-old woman whose husband has since died. "I felt sad, but not because we were losing some great passion, because that was mostly gone anyway. But it had been a sweet and tender part of our relationship, and it wasn't there anymore. When we finally gave it up, it was a relief not to have to work so hard at something that wasn't so great anyhow, but there's also something missing."

Just as in other aspects of aging, some people, more often women than men, accept the loss of sex philosophically, while others go to any extreme to sustain the illusion of youthful vigor and sexual desirability. Most, however, fall somewhere in between, feeling both saddened and relieved, sometimes mourning the loss of sex as they watch it fade out of their lives, at other times accepting it.

"After my husband's heart surgery, it just wasn't the same," says a sixty-seven-year-old woman. "We thought about trying Viagra, but his doctor didn't think it was a good idea. He said a couple of people with heart problems had died after taking it and better to be safe than sorry."

"Is it a problem for you, giving up having intercourse?" I ask.

She sighs, "I don't know, maybe, sometimes it's okay, but then..." She gazes out the window, her brow wrinkling as she searches for words, then, speaking haltingly, "It's like there's also something missing, not exactly the sex itself but . . . I don't know, I can't think how to say it. It sort of doesn't come with words."

It sort of doesn't come with words. I left our meeting with the words ringing in my ears. I know what she means; it's part of my own experience, an experience that until now I haven't even tried to put words to, one whose importance to a relationship I didn't fully understand until it was gone. For most of the forty-five years my husband and I have lived together, sex was there, taken for granted, sometimes great, more often routine as the years went by, sometimes an intimate revelation, sometimes . . . well, just sex. Then it's gone, and something is missing, something I didn't know about before, but it doesn't come with words, just feelings. It's not the sex; I miss that sometimes, but it's not the important thing.

I don't need advice books to tell me to make physical contact, to hold hands, kiss, hug, and cuddle. It's sweet and touching and . . . And what? It doesn't take the place of real sex, and I don't mean just intercourse. I'm talking about doing sex, the fullness of the experience, the variety, the intimacy of a connection that's different from any other, a connection that merges your two bodies, that sets off a torrent of emotion that's unlike anything else, not just because it's sex but because it's relatedness in the deepest sense of the word.

I used to say jokingly, when trying to explain the joys of creativity, that writing a good sentence is as good as great sex. I think I meant it then, when I could still have great sex, but I know now that I was wrong. Nothing is better than great sex, because it's great only when it's an expression of love, intimacy, and relatedness that fills every corner of desire. And not even a good paragraph can do that.

Chapter Eight

The Shrinking Ties That Bind

Two guys I used to play cards with can't do it anymore," complains an eighty-two-year-old man. "One of them had a bad heart for a long time, but it's so bad now, he can't hardly move around. The other one, he's lost it," he exclaims, pointing to his head, "you know, his mind, I mean. Soon there won't be anybody left."

Despite the fact that people of all ages generally rank friends up there with kin as the most important relationships in their lives, friendships are often hard to hold together, at least partly because there are no social rules, no reciprocal set of rights and obligations to bind people together, no public ceremony to honor the forming of a friendship, no constraints to ending it, not even a language that distinguishes the closest from the most distant.

A recent study funded by the National Science Foundation presents a sobering picture of friendship in an increasingly fragmented America. Intimate social ties, once an integral part of daily life and known to be associated with a host of psychological benefits, which translate into physical well-being, are shrinking or nonexistent.[1] One-quarter of Americans say they have no one with whom they can discuss personal problems, more than double the number who were similarly isolated in 1985. And compared with that earlier time, nearly 50 percent more now say their spouse is the only person they can confide in. Although the researchers don't distinguish among age groups or deal with gender differences, it's a pretty good bet that the old are high on the list of those who report dwindling social networks, and that men, who were never very good at intimate friendships, far outnumber women in this respect.[2]

Not surprisingly, friendships in old age are even more complicated and more fragile than at earlier periods in our lives, except, of course, in our teenage years. Then our problems came from being too young, too immature, too insecure, and too slavishly devoted to peer group norms. Now our friendships suffer from the irony that, at the very time we need them most, we too often can't count on them being there: circumstances change, health declines, death calls.

"My best friend for thirty years just moved away because her kids insisted," explains a seventy-nine-year-old woman, shaking her head sadly. "I understand. She's not doing so well, you know, she gets sick and needs help, and the kids have a life. They can't just keep dropping everything and running back here to take care of her. She didn't want to go, kept waiting, saying she was okay, but finally she didn't have a choice. They don't have the money for a nursing home. Not, God forbid, that she'd want to go there. So she's gone. We always said we'd do old age together; now I have to do it alone. I miss her, I mean *really* miss her," she says, wiping the tears from her eyes.

And then there are the friends who die, sometimes in a long and painful death, other times suddenly, with no warning, leaving us acutely aware of our own vulnerability.

"It sure makes you sit up and take notice when someone dies like that," says a seventy-nine-year-old man whose friend died in his sleep a few weeks earlier. "It's really a jolt, you know, a kick in the ass just in case you forgot how unpredictable the whole thing is. You just never know, do you," he concludes, shaking his head in wonder.

When I look back on my own friendships over the years, I see a parade of people who have come and gone. Some left because we'd grown apart and we both knew it, others because one of us moved and there wasn't enough glue to hold us together across the miles, still others left for no discernible reason, except that it's the way of many relationships that pass through our lives. Two people come together for a while, need or want something from each other, get it or not, then drift apart. No words, no explanations, the relationship just eases away almost unnoticed, until one day you wake up and realize you haven't seen each other in over a year. You don't do anything about it, and neither does the other. It seems right to let it go.

Some of my friendships languished because of painful rifts that wouldn't mend, and some, the ones I still mourn deeply, were ended abruptly by . . . Why am I having so much trouble saying they ended when death called? It surely isn't because I fear dying, or that I prefer to speak in the ridiculously ambiguous terms we use for those parts of life we prefer to deny: "passed" instead of "died," "senior" instead of "old." I'm not sure what stopped me just then; I just know it tears at a wound that still bleeds when I'm reminded of the loss. Then there are those friends who came and stayed for decades. They are the women and men who have been an intimate presence in my life, a vital force in my personal and professional development, and who have made my life infinitely richer than it would have been without them. They are the friends with whom I've shared all the pleasures and pains of living—and with whom I've grown old.

But friendships change at this stage of life, sometimes for good, sometimes not.

On the positive side, there's often a renewed appreciation of friends because, in many ways, we need them more than ever before. Sometimes it's because of widowhood: "Since my husband died my friends have become even more important," says an eighty-year-old woman. "At first I was so lonely, I thought I'd die, too, but little by little I began to see some friends again, and that makes it a lot easier. If I didn't have them, I'd just be sitting home alone all the time, and I *would* die."

For others, old friends become more precious with time because they're the ones who share our history, who knew us *when*.

"I've had lots of friends in my life, and I still do. But Rita is my special friend, no one knows me like she does," explains a seventy-six-year-old woman. "It's hard to believe I've known her for fifty-two years. Imagine, *fifty-two years;* we were just kids. We got married pretty close to the same time, and we raised our children and sat in the playground together. I don't know how I could have done it without her. We helped each other through it.

"God, when I think of it; we shared so much. We had plenty of fights, too, but…" Her eyes turn inward as memory calls, then she smiles and continues. "No matter how mad we were, we always got back together. It's funny, I think we've even gotten closer now that we're old. It's like there aren't any more distractions. Or maybe we just need each other again, like we used to when we were young. You lose so much when you get old; you're different, like you've changed, only you're not sure how. But Rita, she was there for it all. She's the only one I can do that 'remember when' stuff with. She remembers."

I listen to her words, and I think about my oldest friend, a woman I've known for nearly five decades, the only friend from that distant past who's still closely entwined in my life, who knew me even before I knew my husband of forty-five years. She, too, remembers. She's the one who knew the person I was then, knew what I looked like, thought like, was like—a version of myself who seems barely recognizable to me now, but not to her.

Unfortunately, not all old friendships fare so well. Some people who are lucky enough to be physically and mentally fit want to look away from a friend, even someone they've known for decades, who is no longer their match. They don't mean to be cruel. It's just too hard to look closely at another's deterioration, too hard to be with someone who can no longer keep pace with you when you walk, too hard to listen to a friend's litany of pain, too hard not to compare the person you see now to who he was then.

I had an e-mail from a sixty-seven-year-old friend recently who is not aging easily. A lifetime battle with the effects of rheumatic fever, heart surgery that weakened her and left her housebound for many weeks, and assorted other health problems have often left her in despair. Knowing I was writing this book and thinking about friendship, she wrote with a breaking heart to tell me about a breach with her oldest friend, the woman who, in her words, has been "the sister of my heart."

"She was the first person I called when my children were born, when I was accepted to graduate school, when I decided to remarry. We have gone through life hand in hand sharing one another's joys and sorrow. This week while having lunch with her, the unthinkable happened . . . I was unaware that my distress, frequently voiced, was getting on her nerves until she snapped at me and said I spend too much time thinking these depressing thoughts. When I protested and said talking helps me to handle my anxieties about aging and its accompanying problems, she said she rarely thinks about these issues and mortality is not a topic of conversation amongst her other women friends. I don't know how to respond to this rebuff. Can it be she fears aging so much that she has to silence me? Do my complaints about aging and mortality interrupt her constructed world where she can avoid these anxieties? I want to ask why my feelings were so upsetting to her, but I fear another attack, so I am silent. I pick up the phone and see her less often now . . . our closeness has been fractured. I am bewildered as to how to reshape our connection. What am I to do?"

When the decline is mental instead of physical, it can be an even more difficult problem for friends. It's hard to know what to do, how to act, how to relate to someone whose mind is no longer agile enough to engage the kind of conversations you used to have, someone with whom you can no longer share your life or the things that interest you. It's as if your old friend were already gone, and indeed, it's true. The person you knew is no longer, the one who replaced him isn't the friend you chose so long ago, the friend with whom you shared so much over so many years.

"We were close friends as a couple and also friends individually, especially with the wife," says a seventy-four-year-old woman who shifts uncomfortably in her chair as she explains her husband's response to an old friend whose mind is slipping. "But the last couple of years, it's been hard. I'm okay with it, but my husband has trouble being around him now. What can I say? He feels bad about it, but it's just too hard for him, so we don't see them much anymore."

Her words strike my heart. This woman, this stranger, could be one of my friends. For my husband, too, has suffered a cognitive decline in recent years, and her words brought to the fore all the feelings I've tried to deny about the changing nature of several of our friendships. In that moment I forget everything I know about interviewer neutrality. Her words hurt, and I want to confront her, maybe even punish her. So I ask with some heat, "What about the wife? She's your close friend, but she gets abandoned along with her husband."

She looks up, surprised at my tone, starts to say something, changes her mind, and finally with a helpless shrug, "Yes, I know, but..."

I left our conversation locked in my thoughts about my own friends, about all the times I've watched anxiously as they squirm uncomfortably when my husband says something that reminds them he's no longer the man they used to know. I've watched also as friends began to slip away while pretending not to. I've had some sympathy for their feelings, perhaps still do, since they mirror some of my own difficulty in dealing with the situation. But in that moment sympathy and understanding weren't enough to quiet the turmoil that brought me up close, closer than I'd wanted to be, to my anger at those friends and my feelings of abandonment.

In a society where age grading—people separated and separating themselves by age—is as common as it is in this one, most old people don't have friends across generational lines. But when they do, the issues that can separate them grow even larger.

Such friendships are most likely to exist among professional people who, in the course of their careers, have become friends with students they mentored and junior colleagues they held a hand out to. I have friendships born in those circumstances, too. But because I was thirty-nine when, along with a few thousand eighteen-year-olds, I entered the University of California at Berkeley as a freshman, the trajectory of my professional development was out of sync with my age and life stage. Consequently, most of my friendships across the age divide weren't initially the product of unequal relationships—an inequality that isn't easily resolved when the balance between mentor and mentee shifts, as it almost inevitably must. Instead, my cross-generational friendships came into being out of shared experience.

In the eight years it took me to go from the beginning of my college career to graduating with a doctorate in sociology and training in clinical psychology, I was surrounded by young people at least twenty years my junior. My professors were my age peers, but it was the students, especially those in my graduate program, who were my real peers, the ones with whom I shared an intellectual life, planned political actions, studied for exams, and worried about term papers. Those students with whom I shared those years were the women and men with whom I would also share the vicissitudes of beginning a professional life. They were all my colleagues—and some were also my friends.

Despite our common ground during those years, we also walked on uncommon ground. I was forty-seven when I got my doctorate; they were in their mid- to late twenties. Some were in the early stages of family building, for others that was still a way off. I was married with a daughter who was already in law school on the same campus I was leaving. Yet it made no difference then, or for many years afterward. We were bound together, shaped by those early experiences and our common professional interests, and held together by affection and decades of sharing our lives, both personal and professional.

But something happened on the way from there to here. Suddenly our lives don't fit together the way they used to. At midlife, they're still working, still striving, still actively engaged in the world, while I'm well into old age and pulling away from all that. My career is largely in the past, as are my ambitions; they're still reaching. As Doris Grumbach notes so pithily, "We become spectators at the show and no longer yearn to be stars."[3] My younger friends *are* the show *and* the stars.

The differences that separate us now often leave me anxious about these friendships, anxiety that may (I say *may* because I'm still not certain what's truth and what's fantasy here) have a touch of paranoia, which recently showed me its unpleasant face. I was with a younger friend when I walked into the lobby of one of the small theaters that dot the Bay Area's cultural scene, saw old men and women sitting in the chairs that lined the walls, and blurted out, "Oh my God, it looks like an old age home"—words spoken with dismay, if not disgust.

It wasn't the words that shocked me, it was the way I said them. *What, I demanded of myself, is going on with you? What's this reaction about?* At the time I wasn't sure; I only knew that I didn't want to be surrounded by all those old people with their straggly gray hair, their wrinkled faces, their bent backs, their walkers and their canes, didn't want to identify or be identified with them.

Later, I mulled over my reaction, brooded about it, wondered why it was so intense. I've never been very good at hiding from myself or denying those parts of me that aren't laudable, so I knew before that evening that I, like most Americans, have an aversion to the old. But why my intense reaction at that particular time? Was it because I'd seen signs that my friendship with this woman, who for a quarter of a century has been counted among my nearest and dearest, had changed now that we were on such different paths? Was it because she, who has just turned sixty and has her own issues about aging, was standing there, seeing what I saw, feeling what I felt, maybe lumping me in with all those old people who were sitting around because it was too hard to stand up? How could it be otherwise? I, we, they—all of us are a look into her future.

I've thought about asking her what she really felt that night as we stood surrounded by the old and infirm (many, I might add, undoubtedly a decade or more younger than I am), but I haven't had the courage. What do I fear? Maybe that she won't speak the truth, and I'll know it; maybe that she will, and I don't want to hear it.

But if that was a paranoid moment, many others are not. Ask any old person who has had young friends with whom they were close, people with whom they shared interests and activities for years, and you'll hear stories and complaints about how they begin to fall away.

"I don't see my younger friends very often anymore," says a seventy-seven-year-old former professor whose eyesight is failing. She pauses, then with the grim humor of the old, "Did you hear that? I said *see,* as if I can *see* anybody these days." She looks away, her eyes brimming with tears, then her voice edged in bitterness, "I guess the fact that I can hear and think and talk isn't enough for them. It saddens me greatly." She's silent again, reflecting on her words, then, "No, I'm not just sad, I'm angry, too. Dammit, I'm no different than I was a few years ago, when I could still help them out. But I've been thrown away because I got old and I might need some help and they're too busy to be bothered."

It doesn't happen all at once; they don't just disappear. It's a gradual process: They don't include you as they did before and hope you won't notice it. They call less often, and when they do, the conversation is just a bit stilted, awkward, less energetic than it used to be, with little pauses as you both search to hold on to a connection that no longer has the same vitality.

You tell yourself it's not you, it's their busy lives that keep them from the telephone, from the lunch or dinner you shared so often before. You remind yourself that they're still preoccupied with their careers, that they have a second family with young children, that their adult children are having problems that engage their attention, that they have new grandchildren with whom they're entranced. But inside you know—or think you know—there's something more. Not perhaps as simple as the fact that you've grown old, but surely a factor.

I was speaking the other day with a sixty-year-old colleague at my art studio who asked how my writing was going. When I told her I was thinking about how friendships change in old age, she fairly leaped out of the chair as the words poured forth.

"Oh my God, I've been thinking about just that because I've always had older friends. They've always seemed more interesting to me than people my age. My closest friends—family really, the only family I've ever cared about—are all ten, fifteen, even twenty years older than me. The woman who has been my dearest friend for forty years is eighty-one now. We've traveled together, lived together, done everything together, and in the last couple of years I suddenly have begun to feel that something is missing, like we don't have a lot in common anymore."

"What do you think has changed?" I ask.

"They're changing; it's happening right before my eyes. It's heartbreaking. They're losing their zest for life. It's not that they're sick or anything, either; they just don't have the kind of energy for living they used to have. We've gone different ways and different things occupy us now. It wasn't ever that way before. It feels like a terrible loss, and I feel guilty. I sit around thinking I'm disloyal and shallow, and whatever other words I can find to berate myself with. But I have to tell the truth: those are my feelings."

Our conversation turns to other things—a new painting of mine about which she offers an informed critique, the larger studio I'm thinking about moving to, her sister's visit—when she suddenly interrupts herself in the middle of a word.

"I've been thinking while we were talking. They're not the only ones who have changed. I have, too. Leaving my job and becoming an artist ten years ago was a transforming experience. For the first time in my life I feel like I'm doing what I was meant to do. It's as if I've finally grown into the me I should have been all those earlier years. Or maybe I should say the person I knew was there but couldn't find before. But these wonderful old friends who I love dearly can't come with me."

We're both silent, thinking about her words, feeling them, each of us with our own understanding of the truth she has just spoken—and our own discomfort. I know she's a warm, generous person; I have been the beneficiary of that as she has from time to time guided my unsure hand as I struggle with a painting. But in this moment, her words leave me upset, maybe even a little angry: *How can she be so cruel?* Yet, I also know it's true; her friends can't join her in her journey. Their lives, their needs, even their desires, are too disparate.

At sixty, she's still in middle age—closing in on the end of it, to be sure, but still there. At that age, most people are either at the top of their game, or they realize they've missed something along the way and need to make big changes before it's too late. True, there's a regretful understanding that their youth is gone, a knowledge that's hammered home by the signs of aging their bodies signal and their mirrors show. But by and large they're still looking more outward than inward, still looking more forward than backward, still hopeful, still filled with energy for living.

In old age, the balance shifts from forward to backward, from outward to inward. We retrench, reflect, husband our waning energy, examine the past, and struggle with the limitations of the future. "There is not time to become anything else. There is barely enough time to finish being what it is you are," laments Doris Grumbach in her book *Extra Innings*.[4] Hope, where it exists, is fleeting; the future sits before us like a dagger at the heart, not only because we fear death but because we're frightened about living—about how we'll live these years, how we'll find meaning now that the tasks that dominated our lives are finished, when and whether we'll fall victim to the many indignities old age inevitably brings.

I see it in my own life, and I see it in others with whom I've talked about these issues. I complain that younger friends aren't as present in my life as they were before, but in truth we are neither of us the same friend we used to be. I'm no more fully present for them than they are for me.

I don't mean I don't love my friends still, but it's not as easy to stay in touch as it used to be now that important parts of our lives no longer match. Where I used to entertain often, pleased to be surrounded by familiar and loved faces while showing off my culinary prowess, I get too tired now to enjoy the evening after a day or more in the kitchen. Where before I picked up the phone easily to touch base, to chat, it's harder now. They're at work during the day, just the time when I might want to talk. By the time they're ready to have a conversation, it's well into the evening, when all I want to do is read my book, watch TV, a movie or whatever other quiet activity appeals to me, and try for the sleep that so often eludes me.

Some people talk about the physical decline that makes it impossible to continue the activities that bound them together.

"Tennis was a big thing that kept me together with my friends," explains a seventy-six-year-old woman. "Until a few years ago, I could beat every one of them in a singles game, even those twenty years younger than me. Afterward we'd hang around the club for lunch or, if it was late in the afternoon, a glass of wine, maybe dinner. Then a year and a half ago I had a stroke, just out of the blue, totally unexpected. At first people came to see me, but it took a long time to get back some mobility, and I guess it got boring.

"I don't blame them; it *was* boring. But it makes me sad. I guess I expected more, but I don't actually know what that would be. I don't have the energy to keep up with them anymore, and I don't even really want to. I mean, I really miss playing tennis, but..." She pauses, looking for words, "Oh, I don't know," she continues, "I'm not the same person I was then, that's all there is to say."

Others say that what used to be fun now sometimes feels like too much stimulation. They want to be with friends, look forward to it, enjoy it, but there comes a time in the evening when they just want the quiet solitude of home.

"I have lots of friends, and I enjoy hanging out with them. But lately it sometimes feels like too much," says a seventy-eight-year-old woman. She looks at me as if waiting to hear what I might say, then, as if I'd asked the question aloud, continues, "I don't know exactly what I mean by that, maybe too much noise in my head, or maybe too much to keep track of. After a while, it makes my head swim, and I feel tired. Not physically tired, just tired of all the talk and the people and...I don't know; I just want to go home where it's quiet."

Friendship, then, presents one of the several paradoxes of this time of life. We want friends, need them as never before, but we're also less tolerant, less willing, as one woman said, "to put up with stuff I don't like anymore." We feel abandoned, an experience that has some objective reality, and are saddened because we're no longer wanted and sought after as we once were. But we can't, maybe don't want to, do what it takes to nurture these relationships as easily as we used to. We want to be in the world, want to have a place in it at the same time that we need more solitude than ever and, therefore, have withdrawn some part of ourselves, some of the energy that was once given over to our friendships, into a quieter, more contemplative and, all too often, lonely place.

Chapter Nine

Hey Folks, You're
Spending My Inheritance

More than ever before, Americans are living into their 90s and even 100s. That's great news—unless you outlive your savings." A reminder from the American Association of Retired People (AARP) of the perils of our new longevity.

For the last decade or so, economists have been telling us that the baby boomers, who represent over one-quarter of our total population, are about to become the beneficiaries of the greatest intergenerational transfer of wealth in history. News that has spawned a growing industry of experts, from banks, insurance companies, and financial planners who want to have a hand in how and where this money is invested, to philanthropies who want to be sure to get their share, to psychologists who have found a new mental health "disease"—sudden wealth syndrome —and have set themselves up to help people through the "trauma."

Depending on how they crunch the numbers and what models of economic growth they use, the experts estimate that somewhere between $41 and $136 trillion will pass from one generation to another in the next fifty years.[1] Yes, that's *trillion*, a number that almost defies comprehension.

Such estimates virtually always generate a lively scholarly debate about the assumptions that underlie them.[2] This one is no different. After a few years of arguments and counterarguments, the researchers who headed up the influential study that started it all published a detailed response to the challenges.[3] In it, they argue that the assets of "wealthy families"—by which they mean the 5 percent of American families with a million dollars or more —will grow enough to support their spending and then some.

Never mind that their estimates are based on the supposition that the various financial markets will flourish, an iffy proposition at best. Never mind, either, that those American families who can actually count up a million dollars have almost certainly included their homes, by far their largest single asset and one that has recently attracted the attention of the financial world as it waits anxiously to see if the softening housing market signals an end to the boom that has been the single biggest factor in driving up the net worth of America's homeowners.[4]

Still, their assumptions about the financial markets holding or increasing their value *could* be right, in which case their simulations probably work quite well—*if,* that is, we're kind enough to die on their timetable. But what if we don't? If we live to ninety or more, how rich do we have to be to have enough money to sustain ourselves and still leave something for the kids? And how healthy? The answer: richer than most of us are, and almost certainly richer than a million dollars, given the cost of long-term care and the reasonable expectation that we'll need it.

"I always expected to inherit some money because my parents have been reasonably well off for most of my life. Not rich, but comfortable and careful with money," explains a sixty-two-year-old college professor. "But now, I doubt it. My father had Alzheimer's and spent his last years, nine of them, in a nursing home. I don't think anyone who hasn't been through it really understands how terrible that is. I don't mean just the financial burden, which, by the way, was over three-quarters of a million, but the human cost. Seeing someone you love turn into a thing, not a person, and there's no way out, it's just terrible, one of the worst experiences in life."

He stops talking, visibly moved, struggles to contain his emotions, then brightens. "My mother, bless her, is eighty-two and doing great. She moved into one of those assisted-living places a year or so ago, and before she was there a month, she was already practically running the place. It's great; it keeps her busy. But it's very expensive. Even with the money she got from selling their house, if she lives another eight to ten years, which right now seems likely, she'll use up her money, and my sister and I will have to find a way to pay the bills.

"That's a big twist, isn't it? You go from knowing you'll inherit money from your parents to wondering how you're going to support them. I don't begrudge her, don't misunderstand me." He hesitates, smiles, then in a voice that mimics an Old West cowboy twang, "Ah'm just tellin' you the facts, ma'am, just the facts."

Not just a clever throwaway line, but testimony to how difficult this subject is and how ambivalent many children are about it. They don't wish their parents ill. But for much of their lives these baby-boom children of the middle- and upper-middle class have known there was a cushion beneath them that would break any fall. They're accustomed to being helped and supported by their parents' generosity and have often lived their lives, made decisions about their own spending and saving based on their expectations of an inheritance. Now, as they watch that promise being washed away by a torrent of expenses related directly to their parents' longevity, they're finding out the hard way that this was a risky assumption.

It's no surprise, then, that even in families where relationships are close and caring, the children can't help being anxious about their own future, can't help feeling cheated, as if a promise has been broken—feelings they struggle to contain, to cover over, to remind themselves and the listener that they're "just tellin' the facts, ma'am."

Writing in the *New York Times*, Bob Morris courageously explores the discordant voices inside him as he struggled to care for his father in the closing years of his life. His image of himself as a caring son, he recalls, his desire to be one, was pushed and shoved by the unwanted thoughts and calculations he couldn't keep out of his mind.

> When caring for an aging parent, irreproachable selflessness doesn't always come easily. . . . My father died recently, and much as I hate to admit it, there were plenty of moments during the last year when I was consumed with an invisible ledger in my brain: my inheritance versus his health costs. Fifteen hundred dollars a week on this, six thousand a month on that. It could all add up to leaving nothing. Not that I tried to staunch the flow, but even thinking about it was an ugly thing.[5]

Where there have been hard feelings from years of family conflict, it's even more difficult, especially when the children are themselves feeling their age and struggling to deal with it.

"I spent half my damn life trying to be her good son and never made it," complains a seventy-two-year-old small businessman. "My brother has always gone his merry way; he never in his life cared about anybody but himself, but he's the one she'll never criticize. Never asks him for anything, either, but I'm her 911, the emergency on-call. My brother still thinks she's going to leave something, at least her house. But I know that was mortgaged up a long time ago, and now there's nothing left and I'm stuck with picking up the tab. I was planning to retire next year, but how can

I if I have to take care of her, too? Makes you wonder about what's in it for us to be living so long, doesn't it?"

I listen to him and remember when, in my early seventies, I was still dragging myself across the country to see to the care of my mother, then in her nineties, and wondering how much longer I'd have to do this. *When do I get to be old?* I asked myself resentfully. *When will it be my turn?* For me, it wasn't about inheriting money; she didn't have any. But the burden of caring for a parent, the reversal of roles, is a difficult situation for any child, no matter how old. When it's a parent who was unloving, cruel, or neglectful, even the most generous can't help being resentful, can't help feeling the unfairness of it all.[6]

The children's concerns, however, are only one side of the story. Parents worry about money, too, about how much they have, about whether they can spend it, about what they might leave to their children. Look, for example, at the T-shirts emblazoned with "I'm spending my kids' inheritance" that sell so well in tourist centers around the world. I smiled the first time I saw someone wearing one of those shirts, thinking it was a cute joke as well as a statement about the freedom from responsibility the wearer felt. But there's an underside to the humor, as there nearly always is, a side that suggests parental anxiety about what they're doing, that speaks to their ambivalence, their need to rationalize, to convince themselves that they have a right to spend their money just to enjoy themselves, that they deserve it. Why else would they need to proclaim it to the world?

Given the history of the older generation, it's no surprise that money is on their minds. Anyone over seventy-five today grew up after Black Thursday, October 24, 1929, the day the stock market crashed and plunged the nation into the Great Depression. Between 1930 and 1932, banks came tumbling down in ever-increasing numbers, leaving millions of families penniless when they closed their doors. The panic, the pain, the terror of those days are seared in my memory, as they are for anyone who bore witness: the shocked silence as people stood in front of the neighborhood bank willing it to open, the confusion when they realized it would not, the surging crowd banging on the doors and windows and demanding entry, the weeping and shouting as if someone had died.

While the Roosevelt years eventually brought social welfare programs to ease some of the pain, it wasn't until after Germany invaded Poland on September 1, 1939, that preparation for war jolted a still-stalled economy back into action. Factories that had been idle were soon humming again, people who hadn't worked in years found jobs, and the Depression was finally beaten back. By the time the war ended in 1945, the United States emerged as the world's only economic superpower, and the next two decades saw the greatest and most sustained economic boom in our history.

These are the large social events that forged the old of our time: the fear, uncertainty, and poverty of the Great Depression, followed by a world war, and then by economic prosperity they would never even have dreamed of. It's an extraordinary story: The parents who now think about passing wealth on to their children are the same people who grew up when more than half of all Americans lived below a minimum subsistence level, when per capita income in 1929 was $750 a year, and when a half million dollars was a fortune. In 1939, when I got my first job, I earned $6 a week and thought I was lucky. Since then, I've gone from a tenement in an immigrant ghetto in the Bronx to San Francisco's Nob Hill—the epitome of the classic American dream.

Not everyone climbed the ladder equally well. Some, African Americans and other people of color, were kept off it by the prejudice and legally sanctioned discrimination that dominated our society at the time. But the war and its aftermath took most of white America up on the flood tide of an expanding economy. After spending our childhood and youth in some level of deprivation, we lived our early to middle adulthood in the postwar economic boom that brought us to working- and middle-class stability, and for the most affluent, our late middle-age and early old-age during the stock market surge of the 1980s and early 1990s that took us into old age with more money than we ever imagined could be ours. I still remember when, sometime soon after the end of World War II, I said longingly to my then husband, "All I want is $20,000 a year so that we never have to worry about money again." And he thought I was asking a lot.

Small wonder, then, that we take pride in being able to do for our children what our parents couldn't do for us, in helping them out when they need it—whether with college tuition, the down payment on a house, or contributions to the grandchildren's education—and now in wanting to leave them some significant inheritance, even if only as a reminder that we were here.

"My parents weren't able to do anything for me; they didn't have enough for themselves," explains a ninety-two-year-old woman who came into old age with about $1.5 million in assets. "I've always thought I wanted to leave something for my kids, you know, something that would help them along after I'm gone, but..." She stops speaking, sighs heavily, then says, "I don't know if I will. Living here [an assisted-living facility] is expensive, and between what we spent on my husband's care and now this, I've already used up a very big part of what I thought they'd get."

"How old are your children?" I ask.

She smiles, "Yes, I know, they're not kids anymore. Funny, isn't it, the way we refer to 'the kids,' when my son just turned seventy-three and my daughter, I think she's seventy-one. They don't really need my money, either; it's just..." She's silent again, looking for words, "I don't know, I guess I just wanted them to have something to remember me by."

Her thoughts follow me long after I leave the interview and contemplate my own feelings about leaving my daughter an inheritance. I'm aware, as the woman I spoke with surely is about her own children, that it isn't money that will help her remember me. Yet something inside me needs to leave her something substantial, something she'll always know came from me. It makes no difference, either, that she doesn't need it. This is for me, not for her, this is my need to say to her, "I'll still be there, still take care of you, even from the grave."

I know that this is more than maternal altruism, that it's my narcissistic wish to mark my presence after I'm dead that's speaking as well. I know, too, that in helping mold her into the woman she's become, I've already left a mark far more indelible than money. And I even know that no matter what material goods I may pass on, my most enduring legacy will be her memory of a tightly bonded intimate connection like no other, an internalized "mom" who, she herself says, will live inside her long after I'm gone.

Why, then, is leaving her money so important to me? The answers that come are vague, inconsistent, unsubstantial—feelings, not words—feelings about my own impoverished childhood, about my mother, who was so weighed down by the need to feed and shelter our bodies that she couldn't think about nourishing the soul; feelings about the fact that I never received a gift from my mother, not when she was alive, not when she died. I promised myself, on the day my daughter was born, that I would be a different kind of mother, give her a different kind of life. Having fulfilled that promise is an accomplishment more important to me than any book I've written, any professional recognition I've received. And giving her this last gift seems the final fulfillment of that pledge.

But I've been speaking until now about the affluent, about children who after a lifetime of comfort feel entitled to share in their parents' wealth, about parents who have the ability to make choices about what to do with their money, who have the luxury of even thinking about their children's inheritance. In reality, despite all we hear about this being the wealthiest cohort of aged people in history, wealth, it turns out, is relative. In this case, relative to how bad it was before.

This is yet another time when we need to look behind the relentlessly upbeat headlines about old age to see what it's about for most Americans. According to the Federal Reserve, half the households with people close to retirement have less than $55,000 in savings, one-quarter have less than $13,000,[7] and median pre-tax family income in 2005 was $46,242,[8] hardly enough to permit the savings that would guarantee a comfortable old age. For people over sixty-five it's much worse: $23,787. True, the net worth of the over-sixty-fives is considerably higher than the median for all Americans, $108,885 versus $61,300, but most of their wealth is in non-cash assets, meaning the house they own.[9]

Presently two-thirds of American retirees rely on Social Security for 50 percent or more of their income; for one in five it's the only source of income. With an average monthly Social Security check of $963 for a retired worker and $1,583 for a couple where both are beneficiaries,[10] more than a few Americans are likely to be eating cat food as the month winds down and they await their next check.

This isn't to say that some significant segment of retired people aren't better off than they were a few decades ago, only that we still have a very long way to go before most old people—especially women and single men, who fare the worst—are able to live moderately comfortably in retirement. Indeed, given how long they're likely to live, even the lucky ones who come to retirement with substantial savings will probably spend a good part of their old age living close to the edge, or falling off it. Small wonder they're busy counting up the years and their money and fearing that the former will outlast the latter.

Forty years ago, it was easy. If a man lived to sixty-five, he could expect to have just three years left. Now the same man can count on twenty. Ask people who are considering retirement and can't quite make the decision and, unless their income is in the stratosphere, almost invariably they'll say their hesitation rests, at least in part, on their uncertainty about whether they have the financial backup to manage the long years that are probably ahead. Talk to people who are already retired, and you hear that even those who have some substantial savings live with the nagging fear that they'll run out of money.

"I used to think we'd be fine when I couldn't work anymore, but I look at it now and see that we're going to run out of money," says a seventy-year-old man who was forced into retirement when his firm merged with another two years ago. "I don't mean to complain; with a few hundred thousand you can't say we're poor, but my wife and I are both pretty healthy, and with the cost of living being what it is and seeing how long we're probably going to live, what we have isn't going to take us very far."

He looks down at his lap, balls his hand into a fist, then continues. "Boy, life's a crapshoot, isn't it. They tell you to prepare, and we did, but now what? It really pisses me off. You get here, and you can't enjoy your life because you're going to live so long." He stops talking again, then makes a noise that's somewhere between a laugh and a cry. "Christ, this is nuts; here I am complaining about living so long. Are you hearing that from other people?"

The answer is yes. For this is another of those moments when the tale of aging in America reveals both a gift and a burden —the gift of years that lies right alongside our fears that we won't be able to live them well, whether financially, physically, or emotionally.

Not surprisingly, I'm hearing the same anxieties from their adult children, many of whom are at a loss to figure out how to take care of their parents while also protecting their own retirement.

"They can't live on their Social Security alone, and except for their house, they've got very little else," explains a forty-nine-year-old man who's struggling to help finance his children's education. "We're the kind of family that doesn't talk about money, but I'm pretty sure they didn't have much when they retired, and I know it's close to gone because they're always worried these days. If they sell the house, which is mostly paid off, they'll have a couple of hundred thousand, but how far will that go? And anyway, where will they live?

"I love my parents, they're good people, but you can't help wondering: How long will they live? My mom's only seventy-two and Dad's seventy-six, which isn't very old these days. If I have to take care of them, and I will, what happens to me and my family? What about my retirement? Who's going to take care of that?"

The answer is: nobody. There's Social Security, of course, but at best it promises a life at the bare subsistence level. It's a puzzle, isn't it? We'll spend untold millions on research to keep people living longer and longer but almost nothing to ensure that they can live those years in reasonable comfort. Until we acknowledge these contradictions and change the policies that flow from them, more than a few children will impoverish themselves to help pay for the care of parents who have outlived their savings.

Chapter Ten

Taking Care
of Mom and Dad

I t has become the baby boom generation's latest, and in some
ways most agonizing life crisis: what to do when the parents
who once took care of you can no longer take care of themselves,"
writes Cathy Booth, a reporter for *Time*, who, in her words, "de-
scended into elder-care hell, when my mother, then sixty-nine,
was found to have Lou Gehrig's disease."[1]

Talk to the children and most will tell you that their aging
parents are a near-constant nagging concern in the background
of their lives. In a 1997 *New Yorker* article titled "The Sandwich
Generation," James Atlas, living in New York, tells of the pleasure—"a sweet moment," he calls it—of opening the door to his
eighty-something parents when they arrive from California for a
family visit.

> But a fugitive premonition occurs to me. This can't last forever. It
> can't even last very long. . . . The Old People, as they call them-
> selves, are always on my mind. When the phone rings, I think,
> This is it. Another stroke, a fall, a lab test with ominous results. I

worry about them the way one worries about one's children. Are they safe? Happy? Do they have enough money? If they fail to call on Sunday, I imagine calamities: They're in a hospital emergency room. They crashed the car....

At first, I was reluctant to bore my friends with these anxieties. No one wants to hear about your children's grades, so why on earth would anyone want to hear about the pros and cons of retirement homes.... I was astonished when, droning on at a dinner party about my campaign to dissuade my parents from handing over their worldly goods to a still-under-construction "retirement community" out in the desert, I found that I had stumbled upon a cohort: the children of the elderly. Middle-aged sons and daughters chimed in with tales of their own.[2]

I thought, when I read his words, that it's something like finding out you have some disease or disorder you never heard of and whose name you can't pronounce, only to discover that everyone you mention it to has either had it or knows someone who has.

The cohort of anxious "children of the elderly" James Atlas discovered a decade ago, has grown exponentially since then, and as the "elderly" get older and older, it will be an increasingly common problem for both the older and younger generations. The National Center for Health Statistics tells us that more than one-third of Americans over sixty-five suffer some physical ailments that limit their activities; among those over eighty, well over half need help in managing at least some of the everyday tasks of living.[3]

No surprise, then, that even a casual mention of aging parents is likely to open up a Pandora's box of anxieties, of stories told with tears, with exasperation, and sometimes, when they can take a step back, with laughter. Not funny ha-ha mirth, but more like the hysterical laughter we all experience at those moments when we're forced to come to grips with the absurdity of life and our own helplessness.

Even if their parents are still doing fine on their own, the children know that their concerns, the "fugitive premonition" Atlas talks about, will almost surely become a reality. True, some children manage to close their eyes to that knowledge, to deny it until it's no longer possible. Sometimes that denial is a response to a history of troubled family relationships; sometimes it's because the children can't bear to deal with the specter of their parents' death. But most of the adult children I spoke with actively worried about their aging parents, often long before their parents need any help.

I see it with my own daughter, who wants me to be in touch when I leave town, even if only for a few days or a week, who calls when she's traveling though she never did before, whose anxiety announces itself over the phone lines when we haven't talked for a while: "Are you okay? How's Dad?" I tell her we're fine, ask her to stop worrying. "It's my turn to worry," she replies.

She and the man she calls her "forever after" have regularly spent about a month a year in adventurous travel abroad. Now, she's reluctant to go away for so long and resists going anyplace where she'll be out of reach for more than a day or two. When I tell her that her anxieties are overblown, that her fears are unfounded, that I want her to go and enjoy herself, she looks at me and says, "It has nothing to do with what you want; it's what I need." A response that moves me to tears, while a little corner of my brain thinks, "Yes, I know, but that's your problem; it has nothing to do with what I need right now."

When she reads these words in an earlier version of this chapter, she calls. "I think you left something out here, Mom." I'm quiet, puzzled, waiting for the rest, until she goes on to remind me that when she phoned to say they were back after their last overseas trip, my immediate response was one of great relief, "as if," she says, "you were holding your breath the whole time we were gone. You actually told me that you were relieved and that you didn't really like it anymore when I'm so far away for so long."

I resist at first, wanting to tell her she's making more of it than I meant. Then I remember the rush of unshed tears when I heard her cheery, "We're home!" at the other end of the phone line, remember, too, how comforted I felt to know she was nearby again, relieved of an anxiety I hadn't even fully known was there.

"But I also meant it when I said I don't want my feelings about this to determine how you live your life," I remind her. "I know," she says, "but that's only because you think you always have to be the mom. I love you for it, but it can be a pain when I feel like I'm getting mixed signals and when you try to protect me when I don't need your protection."

One reader, my daughter's age, writes a marginal note in the manuscript saying, "It would be nice to expand on what you do need. Parents tend not to say what they need, and we children are left to try to figure it out, which leads to problems when we make mistakes."

I think about the question, but I'm not sure what I can say that's helpful, perhaps because I, like so many parents, am resistant to thinking of myself as someone in need. But it's more than that: I actually don't need help with the tasks of daily living. Maybe an errand once in a while, a trip to Costco a couple of times a year for the household paper goods I buy there. But that's because I hate to go there, not because I *need* someone to do it for me. Do I have the right to burden my very busy daughter with something I can do for myself? She says, "It's no problem; I go there anyway." I hear the words and appreciate them, but I don't take up the offer. Why? Because it's my job to take care of her, not the other way around, because I don't want to feel old and dependent, because I don't want her to think of me that way.

But if not such things, what do I need? The answer, I think, is emotional support, a vague idea that I can't easily give content to and that's probably different for different people. I know that more than ever before I need her support and understanding as her father and I try to find our way through the thicket of this new stage of life. I want her to listen, to help me think things through without giving advice, to be present but not intrusive, to be available but wait to be called, and most of all, I want her promise to let me die when I decide the time is right. And between now and then, I want more time with her because I'm so conscious of how little of it is left to us.

These issues between parents and children, the mixed messages on both sides—children who say they want to help but have no time, parents who say they don't need anything but clearly do—are an old story. It's not news either that adult children have always worried about their parents, that they've always cared for them in their old age, and that the role reversal is inevitably a wrenching emotional experience for all concerned. But the cultural context in which this takes place is vastly different now than it was fifty years ago.

Then, few women worked outside the home, so someone was there to care for an ailing parent. Now a changed culture combined with economic need have put most women in the labor force alongside their men, which means there's no one at home to take care of Mom or Dad when they need it. But the more important change lies with our newfound longevity. Then, when people died much younger, caregivers weren't likely to spend as many years on the job as they do now. Indeed, given our extended life span, *middle-aged adults may well spend more years caring for a parent than for their children.*

"My father is ninety-seven years old and needs constant care," says a sixty-four-year-old woman wearily. "He's been living with us for fifteen years; it was okay at first because he could take care of himself. But for the last six years..." She looks away as tears well up and she struggles to regain control, "What can I say? I'm beginning to feel desperate. How long can this go on?

"It feels selfish saying that, but I feel like I've been taking care of my parents forever. First it was my mother. She died of cancer after being sick for years, and I was constantly running back and forth to help. Now it's my dad. He's not poor enough for Medicaid to pay for a nursing home, and we don't have the money to pay for it ourselves or get full-time help for him."

She passes her hands through her disheveled hair, then, "It's something, isn't it? My kids are gone; they don't need me, but I still can't just go live my life, because I have to take care of my father." She stops speaking again, then hesitantly, "I feel terrible talking like this; I love my dad, but..." Her words taper off as she struggles with the thought before she can allow herself to give it words. "There's not much of him left anymore, only the body keeps working—sort of."

This is an overwhelming challenge for adult children of old parents. Those in their sixties and seventies who had looked forward to these years with their promise of freedom from the responsibilities that bound them before, are now asking: "When do I get to live my life for myself?" The younger ones, who at middle age are already stretched thin by their own financial problems, worry about how they'll provide for their children's education, whether they'll ever have enough for their own retirement, how they'll live the rest of their lives, and are asking: "How can I do it all?"

No one wants to ignore parental needs, but unless there are financial resources well beyond what most families can dream about, how to meet those needs is a problem with no easy solution. For the children, it often means bringing their parents into their homes and, among other things, dealing with their teenagers' complaints about giving up their privacy, about having to take care of Grandma or Grandpa, about the intrusion in their lives.

"I've talked to my husband about bringing my parents here to live with us," explains a forty-seven-year-old mother of two teenage children. "He doesn't like it but says he'll be okay with it, although, God knows, I don't know where we'd put them or who would take care of them during the day. My mother can't really get around anymore, and Dad's mind is cloudy, so I couldn't count on him. The girls would have to share a room, but just mention it and they both begin to yowl. We both work, the kids are in school or busy with their homework or their friends, and all the stuff kids do every day. On the weekends, it's a mad rush to catch up with what we didn't do all week." She sighs, turns her eyes from me to her lap, and says wearily, "Oh, I don't know, I just don't know. I feel selfish, but... What do other people do? How do they manage it all?"

It's a situation ready-made to stress some families nearly beyond endurance, sometimes leading to conflicts that fracture a marriage.

"It was hard on everybody: me, my marriage, and my kids," says a fifty-two-year-old woman, her voice clogged with unshed tears. "I had no choice; I had to bring my mother to live with us, but she had Alzheimer's and wasn't easy to live with. God, it was hard. My husband and kids, they all felt like we'd lost our family because everything seemed to get centered around my mother. It got so bad I got depressed and was hardly able to get up in the morning and that only made it harder on everyone else.

"After a couple years, my husband couldn't stand it anymore and left, which didn't make my depression any easier. In the end, I guess you could say we were lucky because my mother died about six months later. Not from Alzheimer's; she was killed by an automobile when she wandered away one day." She stops and stares into space for a moment, then turns back to me. "I've always wondered whether it was really an accident or she somehow knew what she was doing. I mean, did she know she was ruining my life? She was a good mother; she never would have wanted that."

A few weeks after I met her, I spoke with her husband, who returned to the family soon after his mother-in-law died.

"It was like we had no marriage, no family anymore, just her mother and the problems," he explained. "The kids were still home then, and they were as miserable as I was. Someone told us about one of those old people's daycare places, and my wife finally took her there, but her mother refused to stay. I begged Joan to put her foot down and leave her until she got used to it, but she couldn't do it. I tried to understand, but I don't know, no matter what I said to myself, it didn't help.

"Finally, she quit her job and stayed home to take care of her mother, which really did it for me. She knew it would make big financial problems for us, but she chose her mother over our family. I didn't know what else to do, so I left. Maybe you think I was being a heel, but I couldn't take it anymore.

"In a way, I think Joan understood. I mean, she was mad as hell, but when her mother died, she was as relieved as I was, and pretty soon she asked me to come back home and says the whole thing was a mistake now. We never should have brought her here to live." He pauses a moment, then says reflectively, "Of course, I don't know what else we could have done; the fact is we couldn't afford anything else."

If there's one word to describe the dominant feeling on both sides of the bridge that connects the generations at this stage of life, it's "ambivalence." "I love my parents, but..."—a line I heard spoken repeatedly as women and men struggled with the duality of their feelings: their love for their parents, their sense of obligation, the guilt they feel when, no matter how much they do, it never seems to be enough, the difficulty in coping with their own needs, with their jobs, their families, their fears about their future, and not least, the inability to see an end in sight.

"I love my parents, I really do, but there's only one of me," complains a fifty-five-year-old woman. "My sister lives two thousand miles away, so I'm the one who has to do it all, and I sometimes feel I'm being pulled apart by everybody's needs— my husband, my job, my parents. Even my kids; they're grown, but there's always something. My son got divorced last year and moved back home. It was supposed to be a month or two, but he's still here. My parents aren't that old, I mean, Mom's seventy-six and Dad's seventy-nine, but it's like they've suddenly lost the ability to make an independent decision, so they want my help. But it's never exactly right, what I give them.

"I've been reading about how people need to do estate planning, and they said they were interested. So I found them a lawyer who does that, but they won't go back to him because they don't like how he talks to them. I think they ought to sell their house and live someplace where they can get care when they need it, but they don't like the real estate agent I found because she doesn't 'appreciate' their house enough. I spent days taking them around to those retirement places, but nothing is right: this one's too small, that one's too expensive, another one has too many old people.

"You have no idea how much time I spend on these things. I say to myself, *This is your life, Liz, so shut up, do what you have to do, and stop complaining.*" She stops, sighs deeply, "But it's hard to have that constant worry about them, and you can't see the end of it all."

The parents echo the children in form but not content. "I love my children, I know they want to help, but..."—words I heard over and over as parents spoke of appreciating their children's concern while also struggling to retain some autonomy. "I love them; they're great kids, but it pisses me off when they treat me like a stubborn kid who needs to be handled," is the way an eighty-one-year-old father puts it when talking about what he calls his children's "constant nagging."

A week or so after I spoke with Liz, I met her parents, who, viewed from the outside in a two-hour visit, seemed to be perfectly reasonable and quite capable of making decisions. Their complaints were a mirror image of their daughter's. Where she talked about how difficult they are, they complained about her unwelcome intrusions. Where she assumed they needed help finding an attorney, they insisted they were only having a discussion about it and didn't need or want her help. Her father, especially, was incensed because, having accepted their daughter's referral, they found themselves being talked to as if, in his words, "we were kids who needed to learn the alphabet."

His anger still boiling at the insult, he explains, "I don't know what Liz told him about who we are and what we need, but she must have said something to make him think he had to talk down to us as if we didn't have a working brain. It's what happens when you're old, you lose all credibility and people treat you as if you're half brain-dead. It's goddamn insulting, and I don't like it any better when my daughter does it. Take my word for it, you wouldn't deal with anyone who talked to you like that, either. Worst part of it was, when I told Liz why I wouldn't see the guy again, she was angry and blamed me for being difficult."

His wife agrees but speaks with more understanding of the difficult situation they all find themselves in, welcoming her daughter's caring, while also resenting what she calls her "unnecessary" interference.

"We appreciate Liz's concerns, but it's as if she wants to put us in a cocoon, and we're not ready to go there," she explains. "I understand; it's hard for her because she worries about us, but we're not children. We can still decide what's best for us, and right now living here in our house is best. I know she doesn't agree, but that's only because she wants us someplace she thinks is safe, so she doesn't have to worry." She hesitates a moment as if considering whether to go on or not, then adds, "I don't know exactly how to say this, but sometimes I think the kids are selfish, too. I mean, I know they love us and want the best for us, but is it an accident that what they think is best is what will relieve them, whether it's really good for us or not?"

An accusation that's not without some merit, but one also that doesn't take account of the complex and conflicting feelings the children juggle. Looked at from the parents' side, there may, in fact, be something self-serving in the way children push parents to give up their home, their cars, their lives so that they can stop worrying about them. Some even acknowledge it.

"In a way I know I'm being selfish," says a fifty-eight-year-old woman who has been trying unsuccessfully to get her parents to move into an assisted-living facility. "It would be easier for me if I knew they were someplace where they're safe and will be taken care of. I wouldn't worry so much and feel as if I always have to be on call."

But step into the children's shoes and the selfish label applies only if you think of what parents want without considering the price children pay. True, parents didn't count the cost, whether financial or emotional, when they gave themselves over to caring for their children. But parents *chose* that life; it wasn't forced on them by circumstances outside their control. Caring for children *was* their life at that stage, and the legitimacy of their authority to do so was unquestioned. Taking care of Mom and Dad profoundly interrupts the lives of adult children, yet they have no authority to control or manage the situation unless parents willingly hand it over. "I had a life before, now it's gone, and I don't know when I'll get it back—or *if*," cries a forty-eight-year-old woman who cares for her bedridden father.

It's a no-win situation. Parents are irritated when children hover; they resent and commonly resist their interventions. Yet, they are often in denial about the depth of their decline and can't or won't see what's plain to others: they need help. If children back off from the conflict, their parents can fall through the cracks; if they don't, parents are often resentful and difficult. Ancient family dynamics reassert themselves: old conflicts surface ("I never could do anything right"); new ones arise ("My mother used to be a reasonable woman, but she's not anymore"). Where before children struggled to free themselves from their parents' power, now it's parents who are reacting against the power their children try to assert, listening but not hearing, seeming compliant but resisting.

"My husband died and suddenly my kids behaved as if they could run my life," complains an eighty-year-old woman who, while mourning her husband, was also appreciating her first real taste of independence. "One of them wanted to pay my bills, another one was calling me up telling me when to go to the doctor and what I should eat. I don't need them to run my life; I don't want them telling me how to spend my money or how to live. They think because my husband did all those things before that I'm helpless now. It's ridiculous. How hard is it to learn how to write a check? I love them and I don't want to upset them and argue with them, so I finally just stopped listening when they talk. Sometimes when I know it's one of them calling, I don't answer the phone."

It's an upside-down version of the familiar passive-aggressive parent-adolescent child drama: "Where are you going?" "Out." "Who are you going with?" "Nobody." "What are you going to do?" "Nothing." Just as parents must decide when to intervene and demand answers, adult children sometimes have no choice but to take control.

"My mother is furious with me because I insisted she move into an assisted-living place," explains a seventy-year-old man.

"For God's sake, she's eighty-nine years old and has arthritis so bad she can hardly move. How long should she be allowed to live alone? At some point you have to take over, which I did after I came over one day and found her on the floor because she fell and couldn't get up.

"My sister and I tried getting her help in the house, but she either fired them or treated them so badly that they quit. I finally said, 'This is it; we just can't do it anymore; it's ruining our lives,' and I practically forced her to move. I don't think she'll ever forgive me, but there was nothing else to do. No matter what she says, I still think it's the best place for her."

Listening to his story brought to mind a vivid recollection of the impotent frustration I felt when trying to convince my mother to give up driving voluntarily. She'd already had several fender scrapes because her depth perception was no longer acute and her reflexes too slow. But nothing short of taking the keys, which she would never have permitted, would stop her until she nearly killed someone. I don't know whether she would even have given up driving after that, but the question became moot when, much to my relief, the Department of Motor Vehicles took it out of her hands and revoked her license.

Fifteen years later, I confronted the same issue with my husband, who was no less resistant to giving up the keys to the car than my mother was. I couldn't blame him; I know how much being able to go where I want when I want means to me, how much independence is lost when we can't drive anymore. It's one of the hardest issues for a family to deal with—second perhaps only to the decision to put a parent or spouse in a nursing home—especially in a place like California where, because distances are so great, the car culture is practically embedded in our genes. How could I not appreciate what it meant to him? Yet when my daughter said, "You have to do something; Dad shouldn't be driving and none of us should ride with him anymore, it's too dangerous,"

I had the same momentary anger I've heard other parents express so often, the same instant internal response—*What do you know about how hard this is?* the same temptation to say to her, *Keep out*, while also knowing she had every right to step in, and that I had to act.

There are no rights and wrongs here, no black and white; there are only shades of gray in situations so murky that it's nearly impossible for either parents or children to know just when it's the right time to take a step, make a move. Parents who tell themselves they'll know, who promise themselves that they'll take their own lives before they burden their children, often slip past the moment when they can make the choice. For a disease of the mind doesn't arrive like a head cold; it travels stealthily, taking little bits and pieces as it moves through the brain, each one seeming inconsequential in itself until one day the person has slipped over the edge.

Children who think they see the line more clearly, whether physical or mental, push their parents to a decision, mostly out of loving concern but also because they need some relief from the worry and the burden. Parents resist as long as they can, not generally because they don't trust their children and their motives, although that's undoubtedly true in some cases, but because with each step of their decline, they fight ever more tenaciously to hold on to what's left. Their sense of self, their self-respect, demands it.

I'll never forget the anger I met when I suggested to my eighty-five-year-old mother that she needed to move into an assisted-living facility. She paced around her small apartment in a rage, reminded me of every sin I'd ever committed against her, not least moving three thousand miles away, told me that I had no right to tell her what to do, and finally fell back on the silent treatment, an aching reminder of some of my worst childhood days when she sometimes wouldn't speak to me for weeks.

It wasn't until a year later, after several illnesses and a couple of hospitalizations, that she grudgingly agreed to make the move. Seven years later, when she was ninety-two, the director of the facility phoned me to say she needed more care than they were able to give. Always a difficult person, my mother's physical decline, combined with increasing cognitive problems, made her, in their words, "impossible to handle."

When does it end? I thought resentfully, as I dragged my seventy-two-year-old body out of bed before dawn the next day in order to make a 7 a.m. flight to Miami. I'd been making these trips across the country every two or three months for several years, and I climbed into a taxi wondering wearily if I'd ever have one day on this earth without the persistent worries about my mother that seemed to have established permanent residence in a corner of my brain. My daughter, who offered to accompany me, was waiting at the airport gate when I arrived, and I watched her, her head bent over a book, wondering if she would feel the same resentment I was feeling if the day came when this would be her task. I promised myself, not for the first time, that she'd never have to, that I would, in the words of a friend, "turn the lights out" myself before it became necessary.

We spent two days looking at nursing homes, finally settled on one, packed up her meager belongings, and took her to her new "home." Surprisingly, she went quietly, knowing, I suppose, that she had no choice. I introduced her to the director, who showed her around and introduced the people who would be caring for her. After getting her settled and visiting for a while, we prepared to leave, stopping first at the nurses' station to give them final instructions about her care and where to find me. I turned back to her room for a last goodbye and saw her standing in the doorway. I smiled, waved, moved toward her, saying as I approached, "I'll be back soon, Mom." She just stared at me and finally, she whose usual mode was angry shouting, said in an almost eerily quiet voice, "If you saw a dog on the street, you'd take care of it, but me, you throw away like garbage." Words that are imprinted on my brain forever.

She lived in that nursing home for over a year and became progressively more demented, until by the end she could do no more than babble. She was ninety-four when she died after a long, hard, and troubled life. Was I glad when she was finally gone? There's no easy answer.

It's probably always difficult to lose a parent, but a *mother* — the very word conjures images of love, kindness, nurturance. So even though my own mother couldn't by any stretch be called nurturing, even though her rare moments of loving-kindness were overwhelmed by her rage over which she had no control, her death left me with a slightly empty feeling, a child's sense that I was now alone and unprotected in the world. Ultimately, I was both relieved and saddened when she died: relieved because I was freed from the responsibility and she from her mortifying infantile dependency; sad because I could never be the daughter she wanted and she was never the mother I needed; sad, too, because she lived a life so impoverished in human relationships, while mine is filled with riches she could never allow herself to share.

I was reminded of those feelings recently when I had lunch with a sixty-year-old friend who has taken care of his mother for the last ten years. She's been in assisted living for years, moved into a nursing home two years ago, is unable to recognize her only son anymore, and her money is about to run out. We were talking about the difficulties of aging, as I seem to do with everyone these days, when he told me about hearing from a friend that his mother died that day. "My first response wasn't sympathy for Joe," my friend reported somewhat shamefacedly. "It was anger. All I could think at that minute was why couldn't it be my mother? Everybody else's mother is dying, but she keeps on."

How often, I wonder, do even the most loving children have these thoughts? We don't admit them, often barely allow them into consciousness, yet is it surprising that after years of care, after going every week to visit a parent who hasn't recognized us for months, who is no longer the person we knew and cared about, that we'd have such feelings? It doesn't mean we didn't love them, don't love them still; it means only that the person in that bed is not the person we loved.

As the parental generation grows older, their children age, too. Already it's not uncommon for seventy-year-olds to be caring for ninety-year-old parents. By the time the leading edge of the baby boomers reaches their seventies and eighties, they'll have one-hundred-year-old parents to deal with at the same time that they're struggling with their fears and conflicts about their own advancing age.

It's a disquieting thought that raises some particularly difficult and poignant issues. They come to this time expecting to gather the rewards of the years of living. This is their time: they've met their obligations, done what life demanded, only to arrive at this place and find there's yet another demand, one that tosses their dreams into the wind. Almost inevitably, giving up these years to the care of a parent is met with a storm of conflicting feelings as children, on the cusp of their own old age, see their last years slipping by without the pleasures and comforts they'd imagined and planned for.

"This was supposed to be my time," says a seventy-four-year-old widower whose ninety-four-year-old mother lives with him. "Look, I know I'm doing what I have to do, but I never thought when I retired six years ago that I'd be spending my time helping Mom get through the day." He pauses for a moment, then sighing heavily, "It's hard not to think, *What about me?* I've had some heart problems, blocked arteries, you know, and when I think about that, well . . ." Pained, he runs a hand over his near-bald head, then spits out, "Dammit, I could die before I ever have a chance to enjoy my own time now."

In our need to put a gloss on these difficulties, the media have focused on tales of reconciliation, even redemption, as parents and children come together in these last years. It's true that there are moments of pleasure in being able to give our parents the care they once gave us; true also that for some people these years can be a time of reconciliation, a falling away of old grudges, a recapturing of a relationship that had been lost.

"I learned a lot about myself and about my mother in those last years of her life," says a seventy-two-year-old woman. "We hadn't been very close when I brought her here to live with us. I really was afraid it would be a disaster, but I felt so guilty, I had to do it. Don't get me wrong, I'm not saying it wasn't hard—very, very hard—and there were lots of times when I hated her and thought I couldn't stand it another minute. But then there were also times when she appreciated it, and it felt really sweet to be able to do for her.

"Her mind was going at the end, and I don't know, maybe that's why she stopped being so bossy and hard to live with. Whatever, a lot of the stuff that used to make me so mad was gone, and she sort of became like a sweet child. I actually could feel like I loved her again, which I don't think I really felt since I was a little kid."

Even under the best circumstances, however, these are hard times for both parents and children. For the children, these are their *parents*, the people they once counted on to care for them. How do they pay the debt they owe them and continue to meet their other responsibilities, to live their own lives, to plan for their own future? How do they manage the guilt about not do-ing enough, the ambivalence and conflict that are constant companions, the unwanted thoughts that filter into their minds when they're not looking?

For parents, getting old is bad enough; becoming infirm and dependent is the realization of their worst nightmare. Even if they're grateful for their children's care and attentions, for the demonstration of their love and loyalty, their dependence is humiliating at best, dehumanizing at worst. Parents, after all, are *supposed* to take care of their children, no matter how old they may be; they're *supposed* to have prepared for their old age so as not to burden anyone, *supposed* to retain their independence above all else. Anything less is to have failed at the job. Ask almost any American parent what the worst-case scenario for their old age is, and the first words that generally come to them are, "Having to be dependent on the children."

"It's all turned around," exclaims an eighty-nine-year-old man who lives with his sixty-eight-year-old daughter and her seventy-three-year-old husband. "It's not supposed to be this way; it goes against nature. They shouldn't have to take care of me; better I should die."

When I speak with friends and colleagues about these problems of old age, they remind me that things are different in other cultures. In Norway, one friend says, there's something called grandparental leave that affords families—children, grandchildren—the opportunity to care for their elders. I listen and think: *That's interesting,* but how likely is this to become public policy in a nation that doesn't even take parental leave for granted? Or where corporate executives move employees around with less care than they would pieces on a chess board and with total disregard for family responsibilities, whether children or aging parents?

"I did a lot of soul-searching, but I finally realized I had no choice," says a fifty-one-year-old executive who turned down a transfer from a satellite branch to one of the top jobs in the national headquarters of a prestigious company. "Ten years ago I'd have jumped at it, but I just couldn't see moving across the country now. It was a very hard decision. It's a plum job, the one I've been aiming for my whole career, but my wife and I both have parents who are getting old and will soon need our help. We thought about moving the parents, too, but they wouldn't go for it, and the kids—two of them are still in high school—were screaming about it. We realized it was more than we could manage.

"I know it was the right thing for the family, but it's not easy to live with. It's the end of my career here at the company. You can't turn down a transfer, especially a job like they offered, and expect to get the next promotion that comes up. It's not going to happen; the system doesn't work that way. So I'm stuck in limbo here. The only way I can move ahead now is to leave the company, which I'm trying to do, but that's not easy these days, either."

"Yes, but it doesn't have to be that way," says a colleague after hearing this story. "Look at countries like China, where public policy is different and family stands high on the list of priorities." But that's exactly the point. There, both public policy and family culture have historically taken filial responsibility as a given. Parents, children, and the community all have shared the expectation that children will care for parents in their old age.

True, that may be changing now, as China shifts from a rural to an industrial economy and people, especially the young, move to where the jobs are, leaving family and community behind.[4] Still, I ask him and myself, whatever the long-term fate of Chinese family culture may be, how is this comparison relevant in our own nation, whose history is so different—a nation where government gives lip service to family stability but does nothing to secure it and where the bottom line dominates corporate policy irrespective of, and often to the detriment of, family needs; a nation where elder abuse is a problem large enough to merit a front-page article in the *New York Times*[5] on the same day that the newspaper publishes the findings of a report deploring the fact that American communities have few resources for the old;[6] a nation where the San Francisco bus system displays an advertisement about the city's Adult Protective Services featuring a photograph of a battered old woman and a line that reads, "She didn't know her golden years would be BLACK AND BLUE"; a nation where the federal government has remained silent about elder abuse, and Congress considered and failed to pass a bill to create a national database to record and monitor it;[7] a nation where a wealthy son has no obligation, financial or otherwise, to his old parents beyond what he *feels* like doing.

It's helpful to know there are other ways to live, other social arrangements for the aged that are kinder, more humane than our own. It broadens our horizons, puts our own culture into a larger context that allows us to see it and its problems with a fresher perspective. Ultimately, however, comparisons with other societies and ways of being have limited usefulness, since public policies and cultural norms are born in the social history of a nation. In China that history gave birth to a culture where the family, not the individual, has for centuries been the basic social unit, where individuals see themselves as part of a whole that's dependent on all its parts, tied together by social expectations and institutions.

In America, individualism reigns; collective public action is akin to un-Americanism. The family itself stands alone, a collection of individuals bound only by emotional ties, which, powerful though they may be, can also be flimsy when not buttressed by social norms and institutions. Geographic mobility is so common that more than a hundred million American families, give or take a million, live long distances from each other.[8] Success, achievement, a place in the world are individual, often bought at the expense of the whole.

It took the Industrial Revolution to tear apart the extended family of the past and create the nuclear family system that dominates American life so powerfully today. Changing that and the social and economic institutions that support it will take a lot more than wistful talk about how other cultures manage the problems of old age.

Chapter Eleven

Oh My God, We're Old!

How did it happen? When? I look across at him, see the years written on his face, and think, *He's still cute*. An odd word for a man who's six feet tall and weighs 180 pounds, but it's the word that comes to mind. I think back almost a half century ago and try to remember, What was the word I thought when I first met him? Not "cute," certainly, but I'm not sure. Handsome, maybe, big, strong, smart, kind. A hero, a veteran of the Abraham Lincoln Brigade in the first war against fascism: the Spanish Civil War. I remember the evening clearly: July 1961, a party at a friend's house, lots of talk about racial politics in that year when the first freedom riders set forth to test the new laws banning segregation in interstate travel and an Alabama mob set fire to the bus they were on. Opinions flew back and forth, people disagreed, but we two were on the same page, always in agreement.

That's how it began, the initial cement our long history of political commitment and activism, shared even though we'd spent most of our lives until then a continent apart, and still lived in different cities. I had been recently divorced; his wife had died four years earlier. We were young—well, younger. I was thirty-six; he was forty-four, older and wiser, it seemed to me then, filling the space, perhaps, of the father I never knew. The years ahead seemed endless as they do at the beginning of a love affair when anything and everything seems possible; the love of my life, his as well, he says.

Now, here we are. It seems we were young, vigorous, active, then one day we got old. I know it's not true, of course, that it's a process that has been ongoing, that we've been moving toward old age for some years, fighting it when we could, accommodating it when we couldn't. Still, it remained an abstraction, something out there in some future that wasn't really ours, something that happens to someone else, to those old people we see around town who don't look like us.

I send an e-mail to an eighty-three-year-old friend whose body has punctured her denial in recent years, and ask: "How do we know when we're old? When does that knowledge come?"

"There are small steps from one level of recognition to the next," she replies. "But we're in constant denial so that whatever age we're at isn't *really* old yet. Then the steps become leaps, and they come more frequently and are harder to ignore. Still, even with all the stuff I've suffered recently, physical problems that set off my fear that I'd one day be helpless and dependent on my children, it was still *one day*; it wasn't *now*. Then, a couple of weeks ago I was diagnosed with spinal stenosis, a degenerative disease of the spine. *That* feels like *NOW*.

"So when did I know I was old. I feel like saying, I've known time after time that I was growing older, but if there is a moment of knowing I'm actually old that I couldn't deny, it came with visible signs that my bones were deserting me."

But how do you know when there's nothing so dramatic to hammer the reality home? You live with someone, see him every day, but you don't *see*, not really. Sure, sometimes you catch a glimpse, a thought floats through your mind: *He looks tired, older.* But it slips by before you really register it. You don't want to notice, much like the children of aging parents who awaken with a start to the reality they avoided before. Then one day, you look across the room, and it's like an epiphany: *He's old.* It's something like striding along the street, catching a glimpse of yourself in a brightly polished shop window and being surprised at what you see. *Is that really me? Do I look like that? That old?*

"I hear the incredulity about aging echoed by elderly people who seem to be truly bewildered by their forced residency inside their bodies made strangers by time," writes the geriatrician Kate Scannell. "Somehow, unannounced and unceremoniously, old age has snuck into their experience of themselves."[1]

Perhaps it's unconscious denial, perhaps a willing suspension of knowledge, probably a little of both. I read once that someone said, "Inside every seventy-five-year-old is a thirty-five-year-old asking, *What happened?*" I wrote the comment off, thinking it was glib, telling myself that I know very well what happened. But it's not true. For old age tiptoes in on silent feet, taking a little here, a little there, none of it big enough to get our full attention, until one day, it's there, and we're left wondering, *What happened? When?*

"It's like it happened suddenly," explains a seventy-eight-year-old woman who can't get around very well anymore. "One day you're saying, 'I feel great,' the next you're limping around. I mean, I know it wasn't sudden; I had aches and pains for a long time, but I was doing fine. Then one day, I was getting on the bus, and I couldn't climb the steps. My legs just wouldn't push me up. That was the beginning; that's when I *really* knew I was old."

Not that she doesn't still remind a listener that she's "not finished yet"—a remark that conveys her ambivalent relationship to the knowledge she now claims to accept. For while she can no longer look away from the truth for long, she also can't hold onto it all the time. One moment, she's old; she knows it, feels it; an hour later she can still be surprised when she has to push herself up her front steps with the aid of a cane.

I remember how often my mother, then well into her eighties, would go to the doctor to demand a cure for the fact that she couldn't walk as far and as fast as she had in the past. I'd remind her how old she was, tell her it was normal, but it was easier to blame the doctor for neglect or insensitivity than to confront the truth of her deteriorating body.

Now that I'm here, I wonder how different I am. I know better than to expect medical miracles, but I also know how hard it is to come to terms with old age, to understand that those words, and all they stand for, mean *me*. It isn't that I don't know I'm getting old, don't think about it, fret about it, talk about it. But there's a big difference between *getting* old and *being* old.

We see the signs, the markers physical and mental, small aches at first, then bigger ones, moments when memory fails, what we laughingly call "senior moments" as we try to push the significance away. And there are the passing years themselves, the birthdays that have special significance: sixty-five, when a Medicare card drops on your desk,[2] seventy-five, when you realize you've lived three-quarters of a century.

"Seventy-five doesn't make sense," says a woman whose birthday just passed. "How is it possible that I've lived so long, three-quarters of a century? I know it's true, but I keep thinking, it can't be me. I don't remember living that long."

For me it was eighty. I wasn't surprised that I'd lived so long, although because I've traveled so far and my life has changed so dramatically since my childhood and early adulthood, those years seem like a hazy dream, as if they were lived by someone else. The surprise for me was how profoundly something shifted inside me, how quickly a new and unwelcome definition of myself emerged.

Nothing changed, not physically, not mentally, not yet, but I knew it was coming, knew decline was inevitable. *I'm eighty years old! I've crossed the line into old age.* I couldn't get the words out of my head; I'm not sure I wanted to, still don't. It's as if they're the reminders I need to protect against the unpleasant blows I know await me. Not that it has worked. When I notice now that I tire more readily, that I can't walk five miles with ease anymore, that my fingers on the keyboard seem often to have a will of their own, acceptance and denial fight it out inside me as if I'd never said those words to myself.

Five years ago a psychiatrist examined my husband and declared, "Early stage Alzheimer's." Was this the moment I knew he was old? In hindsight, maybe. At the time, though, I was too frightened to think about young or old; all I could think was, *Not that, not Alzheimer's, anything but that.*

It's probably everybody's worst nightmare these days, and for good reason, since, as we continue to live longer and longer, it's increasingly likely that the dread will become a reality. Alzheimer's currently strikes between 4.2 and 5.8 million Americans, a number the Alzheimer's Foundation of America projects will rise to 16 million by mid-century. One in ten persons over sixty-five and nearly half of those over eighty-five currently suffer from the disease.[3] Add to these statistics other forms of dementia not specifically counted as Alzheimer's, and it's a formidable problem for society, for the individuals who suffer it, and not least, for their families.

We went for the consultation because I'd been noticing lapses that seemed more than those "senior moments" we laughed about. So what did I expect? Expect? Want? There's a difference. I *expected* the diagnosis, but didn't *want* it, wouldn't accept it, and pretty soon, I'd rationalized it away. *I've seen Alzheimer's; this isn't it,* I told myself. *It can't be; he's still doing many of the things he used to do, just not so efficiently. So what if he forgets? So what if he, who was the executive chef for his four restaurants, can't cook so well anymore? He's eighty-five years old. Leave it alone.*

I wasn't wholly wrong, because a few months later a review by specialists at the University of California's Memory Clinic challenged the Alzheimer's diagnosis and labeled it age-related memory impairment (ARMI, an apt acronym for the war between consciousness and oblivion that goes on in the brain). I asked how this is different from Alzheimer's and they explained that the personality changes that come with Alzheimer's are unlikely with ARMI. "Unlikely, or won't happen?" "We can't say for sure." "Is it a precursor to Alzheimer's?" "It could be, but we don't know enough to say anything definitively." I kept asking questions until I finally got it: even the experts don't know enough to answer them with any certainty. Still, it made us feel better to get that hated word off the table, and we left feeling somewhat lighter, more optimistic.

In the first years after the diagnosis, I'd watch my husband, looking to *see* something, to get some clue, something to help me understand and accept this thing that, bit by bit, was taking over our lives. But there was nothing to see—a slip here, a lapse of judgment there, inattentiveness, withdrawal, nothing dramatic, nothing that couldn't be written off to mood or simply to normal aging. That's what makes these cognitive failures so frustratingly hard to accept.

"I don't know, maybe the worst part of dealing with Alzheimer's is that it takes such a long time to believe it," says a seventy-six-year-old woman whose husband died of the disease a year ago. "It's not like when somebody has a heart attack; you know they're sick. But Alzheimer's, well, my husband seemed okay for years; I mean, if you saw him, you'd think he was fine. You'd have to be around for a while to know something was wrong."

How do you make yourself believe it when there's no straight line moving in a single direction, no stable place you can count on, when symptoms that are here today are gone tomorrow, only to reappear the day after?

Friends and family often didn't make it any easier. They'd see my husband for a couple of hours, take me aside, and say, sotto voce, "He seems fine to me." "Maybe you're making too much of this." Words that momentarily reassured me but also left me feeling lonely and questioning myself even more than before. *Am I the only one who sees what's happening? Is there something the matter with me? Am I seeing things that aren't there? Making it worse than it is?*

The internal dialogue, the fight I had with myself then—still have at times—was maddening. I'd get upset, angry at what fate had dealt us, irrational anger sometimes directed at him, because anger, which suggests there's something he could do about it if only he'd try harder, is easier, safer than acknowledging that he can't.

The literature on Alzheimer's and other forms of memory impairment tell you that these are all "normal" caretaker responses. But it didn't feel normal, certainly didn't feel right or kind. So I'd gather myself up, move into denial mode, and tell myself I was making more of it than needs to be, denial that was helped along by my husband's refusal to believe what was happening to him. Each time he couldn't manage something on his computer, he'd get angry and insist the problem was mine. "You don't teach me, you just do it," he'd shout about something I'd already explained to him a hundred times. Each time I took over some household function that was formerly his, he'd complain that I was overreacting. "I can do it; it's just not the way you like it done," he'd insist angrily. Leaving me to wonder: *Is he right? Am I being too quick to jump in? How can I do this to this man who prides himself so on his competence? How can I be so sure?*

Then I discovered that our checking account, which he had always managed, was a mess because he hadn't balanced it in many months. *Who have you been kidding?* a voice inside me demanded. *Did you have to wait for something like this to believe what you see? What else will it take?* He asks the same question ten minutes after you've already answered it, has trouble tracking a film or a play, forgets a TV show an hour after he's watched it, can't find words to express the ideas I know (think? wish?) still live in his head. These aren't just small lapses anymore; this is different: *different, get it through your head, accept it, live with it.*

Yes, but it's not always like that, the voice of denial still insists occasionally. He manages some parts of life, goes where he has to by bus, works on the culinary dictionary that has engaged him for the last several years. Sometimes he can even track and remember; sometimes he even reminds me to do something I said I wanted to do but forgot. But it gets harder and harder to avoid knowing what I know.

Talk to anyone who's living with ARMI or Alzheimer's and you'll hear the same tale of the struggle between denial and acceptance, between love and rage. It's easy to pass judgment, but until you've lived with it, you can't know the exasperation, the downright desperation, that can overwhelm any caretaker.

A friend whose husband needs care around the clock calls to say, "I don't know how much longer I can do this without wanting to kill him or myself." We talk, we swap stories, we cry, we laugh, we console each other. I remind myself that I have a lot less to complain about than she does; she reminds herself that most of the time she can still be loving, still look at her husband and see something of the man he used to be. In the end, we hang up relieved—relieved that we can speak the unspeakable to each other, relieved that we're able for a moment at least to feel that we're not monsters but humans who are being pushed to the limits of our ability to cope.

"I couldn't do it anymore; it was too much; I just couldn't do it," cries a seventy-seven-year-old man who had been the primary caretaker for his wife for seven years before he put her into a nursing home. "It wasn't so bad in the beginning but I have to admit, even then I was angry at her a lot. I mean, it wasn't like she was sick or something; she'd seem okay, then she wasn't. How could she suddenly forget how to cook one day? I used to think, maybe she's just getting back at me for something, or she's just mad because I didn't help out enough all those years. Later, when she became crazy and would scream and carry on, that was the worst. You know, you give up so much to take care of her and all you get is a raving lunatic.

"I know it wasn't her fault, but it's still . . ." His words trail off as he fights back tears, then, "My daughter and I went to one of those support groups for a while. I guess it helped a little, but then, I couldn't leave her, and to tell you the truth, I got tired of listening to the others. It's not like anybody can do anything; the damn thing goes on and on, and pretty soon it's like there's someone else sleeping in your bed."

"After taking care of her all that time, what made you decide to put her into a nursing home?" I ask.

He's quiet for a while, then shaking his head, "I don't know exactly. It was after she got really bad and was so angry. She didn't really know me by then, so it seemed more okay. By that time, I didn't even get angry anymore. It was like, What's the use? I just accepted that she was gone, just like they kept saying you have to do in the support group." He stares off into space for a moment, then continues, "It seems like I gave up hope she'd ever come back to me, and that's when I knew I couldn't do it anymore."

He sits for a long time, sad, lonely, saying nothing, pulling at my heartstrings while, at the same time, I can't help thinking that he's among the lucky ones who can say, "I couldn't do it anymore" and buy the care his wife needs. Most people don't have that choice. They just go on putting one foot in front of the other, doing what they have to do, dealing with their feelings as best they can. Which isn't to say they always do it well, as the stories of elder abuse tell us.[4] Or they strip themselves clean financially to meet Medicaid's requirement that they "spend down" all the patients' assets, except for a couple of thousand dollars of burial money, before being eligible for public care. Interesting, isn't it? Our government doesn't allow the necessary resources for living, but you can keep enough money to put yourself in the ground after you're dead.

Is it different, easier to grasp, when the body fails instead of the brain? I've watched others struggle with failing body parts, with cancer, a heart attack, a stroke, and it seems to me easier to accept. How do you deny someone had a heart attack? Or that she's lying in a hospital bed, felled by a stroke? These are frighteningly real, there for anyone who would look. But the mind, when something goes amiss in the mind, there's nothing visible, nothing obvious to hold on to against the denial that comes so quickly into play.

I ask a friend whose husband died of prostate cancer. I see her pain as she returns to that time, now six years ago, watch her push past it and begin to speak.

"The physical changes often come as a crisis and make an immediate change in your life; it's unmistakable. You can't slough it off when they tell you your husband has advanced prostate cancer. You do what you have to do, but you know it's a death sentence. With the mind you really don't know where to draw the line between what's normal and what's not. We've been forgetting words for a very long time, so it's hard to measure. How much forgetting constitutes a major change? With the physical stuff, the line is drawn for you; you can't not know it."

True, we can't deny the major physical crises, but as she speaks, I find myself thinking about the smaller changes that are so common as we age and wondering if it's so for them as well. Most of us are pretty good at stepping around those, at finding ways to live with them, to overcome them, even to tell ourselves it doesn't matter. Still, it's different, I think. We know we're hurting; a wife, husband, partner sees the signs: the limp, the pain, the shortness of breath.

Often we can do something about these things. Surgery gives us a new hip, exercise and analgesics control our back pain. When I notice that my heart is pounding and my breath is short after climbing up the hill to my house, I tell myself that it's not just my age, that I stopped walking up the hills because it began to get difficult and now I'm caught in a loop that's common to all of us. Something gets hard so you stop doing it; you stopped doing it, and it becomes harder still.

If you're fifty, you go back to the gym, promise yourself you'll work out more regularly, which you do, until the next lapse and the next reminder from your body. Yes, I know some eighty-year-olds do that, too, but for me, one of the blessings of getting old was giving myself permission to end my twenty-five-year affair with the machines at the gym. (I don't worry about cholesterol anymore either, but, alas, haven't yet mastered the vanity that keeps me counting calories.) Not that I've become sedentary; I just don't feel obliged to pump iron and walk the treadmill so assiduously. Instead, I walk the streets of this beautiful city in which I'm lucky enough to live, and when I find myself huffing and puffing up a hill I walked with ease a year ago, I plan an exercise program: every day, no matter what else I do, I'll climb a couple of hills—two at first until I get comfortable, then three, then four. I have no illusions that I'll ever again make it from the Bay to the top of Nob Hill, a formidable climb at any age. But this much I can do, this much allows me to say, *Okay, I'm old but it's not over yet.*

It's different with an ailment of the brain, even a relatively moderate one like my husband still has. A person suffering the early stages of mental incapacity usually can't let himself know it, indeed refuses to know it until well past the time when he has a choice about knowing. To this day, my husband still complains to our daughter, "Mom makes me worse than I am."

But even when we know, there are no solutions that work very well: not the medications that can cost a thousand dollars a month and more, not the memory exercises the patient is instructed to do, not the lists he's urged to keep, not the notes a caretaker is expected to write. What good is a note of instruction if the person can't follow it? Or remember to look at it? That's the very definition of memory loss: we don't know what we can't remember.

I put a casserole in the oven before I leave the house to meet a friend for a late-afternoon glass of wine, giving my husband clear instructions, verbal and written, to turn the oven to 350 degrees at six o'clock. Some days he can do it; on this one I come home at seven to a 550-degree oven and a ruined dinner. "I got confused," he says, as I struggle to contain my frustration. He was a *chef*. How could he not know the oven was too hot?

He doesn't, of course. My head knows that, but something inside me continues to rebel against knowing what I know. I *can't* know. Why? I'm not sure. Maybe because if I do, I'll give up on him, and that would be even worse than the self-hatred I feel when I act out my anger.

A friend, reading these words before publication, notes in the manuscript's margin, "But maybe if you do, you could work toward a less tortured acceptance." I think about that and wonder if it's true, wonder if those people who achieve "a less tortured acceptance" don't feel the loss as keenly as I do because they never had the relationship, the level of communication, understanding, and companionship my husband and I had. Is that unfair to others, a rationalization to justify my unruly feelings? How do I know? Can we ever really know what goes on inside another? More to the point, can we ever be absolutely certain about what motivates our own behavior and the feelings that undergird it?

What I do know is that old age comes like a revelation one moment and slips away the next. We move from knowledge to denial and back again in a flash. Ambivalence rules. Part of me knows I'm old, another says *Not yet*.

Something happens: I trip, fall, and get up shaken, not just because I've bloodied my nose but because I have a new awareness of my vulnerability. Old people fall a lot. A couple of hours later, at home, calmer, the bleeding stopped, the humiliation I felt as I lay on the street with people gathering to help fades. Denial sets in: it's no big deal, anyone can trip.

If it's not the body, it's the mind. I walk to my desk for something and forget what I was after. It happens once, it's a blip on my consciousness, twice in a couple of hours, it's a neon sign. It doesn't happen again for a while, the sign fades to a blip.

I get an e-mail from a seventy-six-year-old friend who, after writing about the difficulties of caring for her seriously ill husband, goes on to count up the positive aspects of old age: the freedom, the ability finally to do what you want to do, the time for yourself, for reflection—all the things that can, indeed, make old age a positive time of life. I write back, "How can you talk about being free or doing what you want when you say you can't find a moment for yourself because Jack needs so much care?" "Yes, that's true," she replies at once, "but that's not age-related, that's Jack-related."

I understand what she's saying. If he weren't ill, if caring for him didn't take so much time and energy, so much of her life, this would be a good time. But it's also denial, because this *is* what old age is about—a steady erosion, more for some than for others, it's true, but inevitable as we continue to expand our lifespan beyond what the body and mind can sustain.

Chapter Twelve

It's Better Than the Alternative, Isn't It?

I have a conversation with the eighty-six-year-old mother of a friend who, when she hears I'm writing a book about the golden years not being so golden, exclaims, "Oh, I don't know about that. I think these are good years."

"Tell me," I ask, "what makes these years good for you?"

The question stops her for a moment as she looks for words, then frowning and looking uncomfortable, she half mumbles: "Well, maybe they're not *golden*, but at least I still have my mate; most of my friends don't." Then she brightens and without missing a beat adds, "The best years of life are the fifties and sixties; I really loved that time. Those were the golden years. These years now, what can I say, what choice do you have? You make the best of them because it's better than the alternative, isn't it?"

It's a phrase everyone knows, one most of us say, but it tugs at me each time I hear it spoken so unquestioningly, makes me want to ask: "Is it?" Often I do; almost always it brings a confused and startled response: "You mean you think it's better to die."

It isn't that I'm so eager to die, but I can't help thinking about how destructive our fear of death is, how it compels us to live, even when "living" is little more than breathing, how we have made living, just to be alive, the unqualified objective.

Death, in earlier times, was an integrated part of life, a natural progression from one state to another, feared perhaps, but not denied, not hidden. People could see it, smell it, touch it; they knew its messiness, its meanness, its ugliness—and also its prospect of peace and release. As late as the mid-twentieth century, only 50 percent of Americans died in the hospital; the rest died at home. A mere twenty years later, the figure had jumped to 70 percent, and today it's up to 80 percent and still climbing.[1] Consequently, most Americans have never stood in the presence of death, never watched its awesome power and majesty as it took a loved one's last breath.

The whole untidy process of dying is now the province of medical experts who, with their technology, aid and abet our denial of death. It comes back to us as part of a ritual—a wake, a funeral—where we see only the embalmed, beautified body or the closed casket hiding it away. It's like listening to a story about death, a tale of a medical failure. "What a shame," people will say at a funeral. "They tried everything and nothing worked." Implying that there should be something that "works," some machine, something, that will confound death.

Long before her death, Susan Sontag, a brilliant, accomplished woman whose words were always brimming with clarity and unflinching honesty, wrote of death as "the obscene mystery, the ultimate affront, the thing that cannot be controlled. It can only be denied."[2] A belief she lived out to the last moments of her life.

In a moving article, Ms. Sontag's son, David Rieff, pays homage to his mother's courage as she fought and won, temporarily at least, two previous cancer assaults before the last one ended in her death.

My mother was determined to try to live no matter how terrible her suffering...[Her doctor] offered her the option of treatment with a drug...which gave many M.D.S. patients some months during which they felt relatively well. But the drug did little to prolong life. My mother replied with tremendous passion, "I am not interested in the quality of my life."[3]

Tears stung my eyes when I read it, tears for this woman I had so admired who, despite the warnings from doctors that more aggressive treatment was "medically futile," willingly submitted herself to torture just to live for another day, another week, another month.

I thought about my response for a long time, torn between whether I saw her as courageous or in the grip of fear and denial. Where's the line between the two? Is there one, or do they inevitably coexist? After all, she battled death to a temporary standstill twice before. Why shouldn't she try to do it again? How much of a chance justifies continuing the fight: 5 percent? 1 percent? At what point is the chance so small that it's medically irresponsible, even unethical as some physicians argue?

I have no answers; only more questions. I say firmly now that I want no part of a diminished life or one filled with pain, that death in such a condition would be an easy choice for me. But at what point will I decide that my life is diminished enough? Can I know now what will *feel* sufficiently impaired to me? Or will I find, when I'm actually walking down that path, that each crossroad I come to doesn't feel quite bad enough until, as has happened to so many others, I've crossed over the line to that place where I'm no longer capable of making the decision?

I write to a friend with whom I've been discussing these issues for some time and who's more on the side of fighting for every day of life than I am.

"I don't think I'd ever give up the fight to live," he writes. "It's either that or nothingness, and who can tolerate nothingness? I simply can't imagine myself not *being*, it's impossible to conceive. It isn't just denial of death, it's an affirmation of life."

His reply puzzles me. How can it be an affirmation of life when someone is in intolerable and incurable pain, when the mind is no longer fully functional, when the body can't do for itself the basic things necessary to sustain life? Is it affirming life or fearing death that drives people to fight for every breath?

"I actually don't understand what you're talking about," I write back. "Doesn't the quality of life mean something? If I'm tired and weak and worn out and hurt, why would the idea of nothingness fill me with such anxiety? Why wouldn't it feel like a blessing?"

He replies, "Okay, so for you the quality of life is what counts. But where do you draw the line? How terrible does life have to be to exchange it for eternal nothingness? If you can deal with that nothingness, you're a better man (pardon the gender confusion) than I am."

Then, in a postscript later that day, he writes, "I've been thinking about our conversation and, to tell you the truth, I think I'd change places with you if I could. Yours seems the easier road."

Which is easier, which harder? I don't know. What I do know is that life is full of potential, of possibilities, of promises that we're loath to give up, and that so long as we're alive we can tell ourselves we're the agents of that life, believe in the illusion that we're in control. I know, too, that death is the great unknown, the mystery we'll never solve and which, if we dare to look it in the face, offers only the terrifying realization of our helplessness. It signals the end—the end of possibility, the end of promise, the end of our very physical being—and leaves behind only a vast unknowable emptiness.

Does this make life worth living at any cost? Is it living when we're so incapacitated that we're incapable of caring for our most personal and fundamental needs? Most people say no, adding that their deepest wish is for "a good death," by which they mean one that's quick and painless. Tell any seventy-year-old that someone died of a heart attack in his sleep and it will strike both fear and hope in his heart—fear that he could be next; hope that if he is, death will come as quickly and painlessly. The worst possibility, far more frightening than dying itself, they say, is a lingering death, where pain is unremitting and they're hooked up to machines that keep them alive to no purpose.[4] I have no doubt they mean what they say, but ambivalence reigns in death as well as in life, and when the question arises, so do the fears and the conflicting feelings.

"I know what I want and what I don't want," asserts a seventy-eight-year-old man suffering from heart disease. "I've told my family and my doctors: I want them to do what they can, but if they have to put me on machines to keep me alive, I don't want it. I don't want to be in a coma and a vegetable or anything like that *unless there's a chance that I could come around and be normal again* [emphasis mine]."

And in that "unless" we see his ambivalence. He wants to take control of his death, but how can he be sure he or anyone else will know when it's the right moment? So he hesitates, says "unless" as he tries to foreclose any mistakes, which leaves his doctors without a mandate and his relatives, already wishing to forestall his death, hesitant about making the decision to pull the plug. For who can know with absolute certainty that he'll never "come around and be normal again"?

True, there are differences among people. On hearing that there's one last-chance experimental procedure for a cancer that has metastasized beyond the reach of tested therapies, one seventy-five-year-old pleads, "Do whatever it takes, just save my life," while another says, "No, I'll take the months I have and live them." But even when people make the decision to forgo treatment, it's almost never without mixed feelings—conflict that's fed by a medical establishment for whom any death is a failure and by a family that wants to hold on for just a little longer.

More than a few of the people I met in the course of doing this book—some who were ill and infirm, some who were not—spoke with a compelling and authentic voice about being weary of living, saying that "life is just too long," that they're "tired and ready to go," that they want "to lay down and rest." "It's like God forgot about me. What's he waiting for?" demanded an eighty-nine-year-old woman who can no longer care for herself.

I was moved by their words, knew that part of them meant what they said, but the other part, the side that resists death, was plain for anyone who would look to see. All were in assisted-living facilities that are dedicated to saving their lives; all, in the year or two before we met, had some medical procedure that promised—a promise often unfulfilled—either to make them feel better or to extend their lives a bit. When I remarked upon the incongruence between their words and deeds, some said their doctors convinced them to do it, others explained that they gave in to pressure from family members, and a few acknowledged that at the last moment they were too afraid not to do it.

Would they have been able to forgo these treatments if they hadn't had pressure from others? They can't know, nor can we. What we can know is that the fear of death, the terror the very idea inspires, is a near-natural consequence of a society so committed to its denial that the alternatives that might allow for a different choice don't get much serious consideration, either by the medical establishment, the family, or the patient. As one eighty-eight-year-old man puts it, "When I came right up to it, I guess I was too scared not to try to put it off."

"Would you do it again?" I ask about the surgery from which

he had not yet fully recovered and that arguably left him no better than he was before.

"I sure hope not," he says with as much certainty as he can muster.

We say we want to die with dignity and mean it, but we're so frightened of death that we submit to often painful and undignified medical procedures in the often vain hope of putting off our meeting with it just a little longer. We say we want to control our death, but hope triumphs over reality, and we give over both life and death to the technicians' machines and the surgeons' knives.

But what about people who are deeply religious, who believe in an afterlife in which they'll be reunited with loved ones? Wouldn't they go more readily into death than those who don't hold that faith?

I'm certain their belief helps them through difficult times, and I have sometimes envied the comfort religious people find in their faith. I have no doubt, either, that there are women and men who believe that their impending death is God's will, that they'll find the peace and joy in death that escaped them in life, and who go as calmly and peacefully as possible into that better life.

"I had a brother who died in a motorcycle accident when he was sixteen, and my mother never was the same after that," says a fifty-nine-year-old woman, speaking about her mother's death. "She was very religious, so she believed God had some reason for taking him, but it didn't really make it easier for her to live with it. She got very emotional and was depressed most of the time after Robbie died." She heaves a sad sigh as she remembers. "It changed our lives. I don't think she ever had a happy day from the time he died until she did. When she knew she was dying, she kept thanking God for taking her so she could be with her son again, and when she finally left us, she looked . . . what do you call it . . . euphoric."

But at least from the stories I heard from others about their parents' death, most believers generally don't seem any more eager to rush off to death than those lacking in faith.

"My father died five years ago and after that my mother always talked about wanting to die so she could join my father up there and live in eternity with him," says a fifty-seven-year-old woman. "But it's funny, because when the doctors told us she had maybe a month to live, she wouldn't sign the DNR [Do Not Resuscitate] order, so she spent six months hooked up to machines."

"What do you make of that?" I ask.

"I'm not sure. I never understood why she didn't just sign it or later on, when she was still conscious, why she didn't let them turn off the machines. It was what she said she wanted the whole time after my father died, but when the time came, she couldn't do it. She said things like, 'It's God's will; he'll know when.' I have to admit, I wondered if God hadn't already told her and she just couldn't hear him, because otherwise why would she be so sick and dying. But I didn't feel like I could say anything. Anyhow, it wasn't God who finally turned off the machines, it was the doctors."

She's quiet for a moment, thoughtful, then says with a sigh, "I guess it's never easy to die, even though you believe you're going to a better place. When it comes right down to it, how do you *know?*"

I left her thinking about my mother, who in the years before she died complained endlessly that she had lived too long, that she'd had enough, that there was no pleasure and no reason to keep on.

"Why doesn't God take me?" she'd ask plaintively before she slipped over the edge and couldn't ask anything anymore.

After hearing the same wish every time I visited, I decided she must mean it, and asked, "Mom, would you like me to help you die?"

She looked at me angrily. "What, you want to kill me?"

"No, I want you to live or die as you see fit, and you keep telling me you want to die. All I'm asking is if you want me to help."

"God doesn't need your help; he'll know when it's my time."

In fact, he didn't. She died of pneumonia, the disease caretakers call "the old people's friend," but not before I told her doctor to keep her comfortable but not to medicate her. Would she have died right then anyway? Her doctor thought she would, but when I asked for guidance, the best he could say was, "I think it's the right decision, but we can never be sure."

Some people talked actively about suicide as a means of taking control of both their lives and their deaths. Several told me that they had given clear instructions to their families not to interfere when they decided the time was right. Brave words. But despite suffering serious infirmities, they were still alive, still engaged enough to agree to talk to me, still not ready to take that final step.

"I'm waiting for the right time to do it," says a very frail ninety-one-year-old woman, explaining how she's saving pills.

"Do you have some idea when that time might be?" I ask.

"My body may be weak, but up here [pointing to her head], this works fine. So I guess the right time will be when that begins to go." She pauses a moment, looks at me with a rueful smile, and says, "I know, everyone says that, then they wait too long and can't make the decision anymore. I see it around here all the time."

A recent report from Oregon's Department of Human Services, the only state in the union that has legalized physician-assisted suicide, is instructive.[5] Despite the fears of those who opposed the law because they believed the state would be swamped with suicides, only sixty-four prescriptions were written for death-dealing drugs in 2005. Of those, only thirty-two people actually chose to die and took the medication. Fifteen of the remaining thirty-two died naturally of their illnesses, seventeen were still alive at the end of the year, and six people who had been given prescriptions in 2004 took the medication and died in 2005, making a total of thirty-eight physician-assisted deaths that year. Statistics that tell us a good deal about the complexity of our relationship with death, even when we think we want it.

We can't know without asking them why people who had prescriptions would choose to wait for death without offering it a helping hand. The reasons, I'm sure, are complicated and probably weighted differently for each of them. But the one common factor was the knowledge that living or dying was in their control, that they could act when they decided the time was right. Given that so much of our anxiety about death is the uncertainty with which it makes its appearance, the pills in hand offered the assurance of certainty that made it possible to put off acting. This, the issue of control, the power to decide when it's enough, is what fuels the right-to-die movement, a movement that I expect will grow rapidly as the baby boomers, who have demanded and won control of their lives in other arenas, move into this next stage.

It's hard to imagine a time when the end-of-life decision, whether the patient chooses to make it or the family is forced to, won't be filled with conflict and ambivalence. But when, as is true in this country, there's neither public policy nor community agreement to support the decision to end a life, the field is wide open to the kind of acrimony we saw in the national furor over the Terry Schiavo case, where the courts were forced to decide whether or not to keep the machines pumping.

Ask anyone who has had to make the decision, and you'll hear stories about how hard it is, even from people who are true believers. Ask any physician, and you'll hear tales of family conflict that testify to the difficulty. Speaking of a seventy-four-year-old woman with a long history of diabetes and all the problems that attend that disease, a doctor explains:

"Her heart finally was giving out; it happens; there's not much we can do about it at that stage. We brought her back a couple of times, had her on life support, but it was pretty clear she wasn't going to make it, and I told the family so. It's a hard time for a family, even if they're together on the decision-making, but when there's a difference, it can break your heart and theirs. In this case, the husband came in two days later and said he was ready to pull the plug but wanted to wait for the daughter to arrive from out of town.

"They were all there when I came in that evening, but the daughter had told her father she'd never forgive him if he gave the order. Everyone was in tears; the poor man didn't know what to do; the daughter was crying hysterically, saying, 'You can't kill Mom; I won't let you.' He was saying, 'She's already dead; this is what she wanted.' The two other kids were trying to calm the others down, but weren't even getting to first base. They just have to work it out, or the person who has the power has to make the decision and take the consequences. It's not easy."

As I listen, my anger rises: Who is this daughter doing this for? Her mother or herself and whatever unfinished business she thinks they may have? What right does she have to threaten her father when she'll go home to her life and family, while he's consigned to what could be a long nightmare? Thoughts that are followed almost immediately by a cautionary voice that reminds me to be careful, that I have no right to judge how a person responds in such circumstances. The emotional temperature in a family, never fully stable, flares quickly when confronted with hard decisions, none more difficult or painful than the one that asks us to have a hand in the death of a loved one.

We question our own motivations, look uncertainly at what prompts others who want to make a different choice. Simmering rivalries, long-buried conflicts, all the angers, regrets, and disappointments that are the almost inevitable accompaniment of family life—all these rise to the surface as a family confronts the questions: Is death inevitable? Is this the time? Should we wait? Our own fears of death step in, denial strengthens: There could be a miracle; it's happened before.

"What role can a doctor play in such wrenching conflicts?" I ask.

"It depends on the doctor. I believe that making a person as comfortable as possible and not extending life beyond what's reasonable is the most ethical way. But there's a lot of discussion and controversy about that right now, and different physicians make different choices. We're trained to save a life at all costs; that's what we do; that's what we swore to when we took the Hippocratic oath, so these decisions aren't easy for us either. All we have to go on is experience and the best reading of the scientific evidence. But in the end, it's art that tells you when to make the decision, not science. A doctor can only advise.

"In this case, there was another sister and a brother who played a mediating role and a couple of days later convinced their sister to go along with the program. Unfortunately," he concludes with a heavy sigh, "it doesn't always work that way and the hard feelings sometimes aren't ever resolved."

In an article titled "The Last Word on the Last Breath," Jan Hoffman raises the issue of who should have the last word: the medical experts or the patient's family?[26] It's not an easy argument to settle, since there's something to be said for both sides.

In the decades before the upheavals of the 1960s questioned all authority, from the highest office in the land to the family doctor, decisions about life or death, if one was to be made, were the province of the physician. The doctor knew best. He (and it was nearly always a "he" then) was held in near-God-like esteem, the expert, the wise man who cared only for his patients' welfare, the man to whom people turned for advice, who held their lives in his hands, who knew their bodies better than they knew them themselves. The patient's need to know was at the physician's discretion. Rarely were patients told the truth about their condition, especially if it were serious enough to suggest the possibility of death. Death and dying were ruled out of patient-doctor discourse; euphemism and false promises were the mode of the day.

Since then, the doctor has been flung from his lofty perch, replaced by medical technology, and the patient or an appointed surrogate rules. We demand the truth; we have laws requiring informed consent, make living wills to instruct our physicians about what we expect in our dying days, and resort to lawsuits to enforce those wishes when they are violated. A threat that weighs heavily on every doctor who's called upon to make the tough decisions.

Read what doctors write, listen to what they say, and you'll hear tales of decisions made, not on their best medical judgment but on their fears of a lawsuit. They may know in their hearts that there's nothing left to be done: the patient has been intubated, injected, studded with electrodes, shocked, and had a central line inserted into his groin. But when the patient's relatives insist it's not enough, visions of a malpractice suit and censure by the hospital's ethics committee own the day. Medical judgment is set aside, action takes over, even though they know it's not just futile but brutal. "One way or another," writes Sherwin Nuland, "the rescue credo of high-tech medicine wins out, as it almost always does."[7]

"Kneeling on that bed, doing CPR, felt not only pointless, but like I was administering final blows to someone who had already had a hard enough life," said a young physician, recalling his first such experience. "Why was I forced to crack this person's ribs? Why couldn't we let the patient die in peace?"[8]

I'm not advocating for a return to the doctor-knows-best days, only for some balance, for something that looks more like a partnership where a doctor respects our needs and wishes and we respect his expertise, where we trust her best judgment at least enough to look inside ourselves, to examine our motives carefully and ask: Is our pain at losing a loved one combined with our fear and denial of death running the show?

"My father was in a coma and brain-dead; he was being kept alive by machines. I knew we had to turn them off, but my mother just couldn't let go," says a fifty-eight-year-old woman, tears flowing down her cheeks as she lived once again the impossible bind she found herself in. "She kept saying we didn't know, miracles happen, she couldn't kill him. The doctor tried to talk to her; he knew we had to end it, but she wouldn't listen.

"At one point, I asked the doctor if he just couldn't do it when we weren't there, but he couldn't; he said it was illegal because my father hadn't left any DNR instructions. But how could he? One minute he was fine, the next he was out of it, gone away before he had a chance. I know some doctors do things like that, like help out people in the end, but this guy wouldn't, and my mother just wasn't going to do it no matter what anyone said. She just sat there day after day insisting that some miracle would bring him back." She pauses, trying to contain the anger she still feels, then sighs. "My dad lived on those damn machines for eight more months before he finally died. What a waste!"

Multiply this story by the thousands and we see enormous waste—emotional waste, waste of social resources, waste of medical expertise. What is it that compels us to spend billions of dollars to keep people alive—no, not alive, breathing—while we let children go hungry?

In *The Denial of Death*, Ernest Becker's classic on death and dying, he argues that we are haunted by an "all-consuming terror" of death, "that it is a fear that is natural and is present in everyone, that it is the basic fear that influences all others, a fear from which no one is immune, no matter how disguised it may be."[9] But I wonder.

It may be true that death is a feared and alien monster in all modern Western societies, that we Americans are not unique in our insistent denial of death, in how much it is hidden away from common view, in our reluctance to even speak the word, crouching instead behind tired euphemisms like "passing" and "going over to the other side." But is it, as Becker asserts, a universal fear, "natural and present in everyone?" Or is our denial of death a product of a society that has the hubris to believe it can defeat it?

There's no evidence that the old in preliterate societies, who sometimes are left to die when the tribe must move on, fear death as we do. Quite the opposite. It's what they expect, probably have prepared for as part of the social compact to ensure the tribe's survival. Nor do most Eastern beliefs about death suggest the kind of pervasive fear we know.

"In India it's very different, not at all the same as it is here," explains an India-born man in his mid-sixties. "People prepare for death. That's what the last twenty years of life is supposed to be about, preparing to withdraw from worldly attachments. I don't mean people don't take care of their responsibilities, but while they're doing that, they're also in an active process of withdrawing from *maya*, which means *this* world, and moving toward the spiritual world. The idea is that an attachment to life, *maya*, prevents us from entering the spiritual world, which, for us, is the real world."

"Yes," I remark, "but isn't it also easier to accept death because you believe in reincarnation, that you'll come back one day, even if as something else? That doesn't feel as frightening as the nothingness we in the West fear."

"No," he says with a laugh, "you've got it all wrong. I remember a cautionary tale I heard from my mother when I was a child: A dying man saw a fly land on an apple and lick it, and he thought: I wish I were a fly. He died and came back as a fly. That's what happens when you're not fully detached from *maya;* you come back and have to continue to suffer life's disappointments and pains. Being reborn is being condemned to *maya;* that's just what you don't want. You want to detach yourself so much that your soul will not come back. You want to attain *nirvana,* a state of non-being, or *moksa,* which is another word for the same thing."

They search for nothingness, for non-being, the very thing that frightens us most—the difference, it would seem, between Western materialism and Eastern spiritualism.

The Belgian poet Maurice Maeterlinck writes, "We deliver death into the dim hands of instinct, and we grant it not one hour of our intelligence."[10] Perhaps we instinctively recoil from death; certainly Ernest Becker thought so. But it seems to me that the terror with which we approach death is at least partly learned, born of the reverence we give to the corporeal body, the primacy of the material self, rather than the spirit. Given those fears, it's true that reason too often is replaced by anxiety in our contemplation of death.

Yet reason doesn't always give us the answers we seek. So, much as I value reason, I can't help wondering how it happens that some people manage to outwit death, even if only briefly. A friend, whose mother had been on a respirator for some years, told me recently that she died only after he "gave her permission to go."

"I told her that I loved her very much, that she'd been a wonderful mother and I'd never forget her, and that I'd miss her. And I also assured her that my brother and I would be fine, and if she wanted to die, we'd be right there with her. Within minutes after I finished saying what I had to say, she heaved her last breath."

We've all heard such stories: people who hang on to life with amazing tenacity just until they can witness some long-awaited event—a daughter's wedding, a grandchild's Communion, a son's bar mitzvah, a prodigal child's return to the family, or in this case, a son's reassurance that he didn't need her to live—then die almost immediately afterward. No one knows how people manage to defer death in these situations. Will plays a part, certainly, but if will alone could do it, no one would die.

Death is a mystery with its own pace and its own time frame. It's the ultimate unknowable, the only act of life besides birth against which we are totally helpless. Our defense has been to deny it, to obliterate it from consciousness. We're like a small child playing peekaboo. She covers her eyes, shuts out the world, and believes it can't see her. But the world sees her, just as death finds us no matter where we hide.

In his foreword to *The Denial of Death,* Sam Keen observes that if we have the courage to face it, "the contemplation of the horror of our inevitable death is, paradoxically, the tincture that adds sweetness to mortality."[11] When we shrink from the inevitable, when we capitulate to fear and denial, we forfeit some of the pleasure of living for the illusion of immortality and cheat ourselves of what it means to be fully alive.

When I started this book, I thought that these lines from Dylan Thomas's famous poem would be its epigram:

> *Do not go gentle into that good night,*
> *Old age should burn and rave at close of day;*
> *Rage, rage against the dying of the light.*

I've always admired these words, always thought they were dead-on, the perfect expression of my own feelings about old age. But whatever anyone learns from reading a book, the author learns more from writing it.

I know now that it's one thing to "burn and rave" at old age, another to do so "against the dying light." I understand for the first time how much our fight against the "good night" costs, how our fear of death imprisons us, how it invades, no, contaminates, our life, how our denial of it closes us off from the full affirmation of the life we could be living.

To live and die with dignity means to give up our denial of death, to accept it as part of life, linked to it as inevitably as the night follows day. Only then can we leave behind the fear and confusion that now assaults us and that deprives us of the full appreciation of the mystery of both life and death. As Sherwin Nuland writes so pithily, "The dignity that we seek in dying must be found in the dignity with which we have lived our lives.... The art of dying is the art of living."[12]

Chapter Thirteen

One Last Word

To know how to grow old is the master-work of wisdom, and one of the most difficult chapters in the great art of living."[1] This whole book has been about the difficulties of finding the way to that masterwork of wisdom. Until now we who are old were tethered to society through a series of institutions—school, work, family, church, community—that structured our lives, defined our place in the world, and gave shape to our identity. We had goals then, destinations to which we looked forward, things to accomplish that gave life its meaning. But as Freud noted a long time ago, a strange thing happens when we meet success. Instead of entering into that subjective state of grace we expect it to bring, we often become unsettled, feeling adrift, as if something has gone out of life.

Freud thought such feelings were a response to the guilt we experience over our good fortune. Perhaps so, but it surely isn't that simple. For this is one of those times when winning and losing are opposite sides of the same coin. We finally achieve a long-sought goal—raising the children, getting a promotion, paying off the mortgage, winning the gold (actually or metaphorically) —and instead of the unambiguous joy of accomplishment, we feel something else, an emptiness where the goal lived, a sadness that suggests loss. And with it the emerging understanding that it's not the destination that has given life its meaning and continuity but the journey itself.

This is the dilemma of the new old age. The journey continues, but to what end? Perhaps it was easier when "old" meant sixty-five and few who reached that age lived much beyond it. But when half the sixty-five-year-olds today can expect to see eighty-five, "old" becomes far more complicated both socially and personally.

The years have left us wise in many ways, but growing old gracefully when we live so long generally is not one of them. How, then, do we go about creating this masterwork in a society that has so little use for us? Stay physically healthy, keep mentally alert, and engage with life, the gurus of aging exhort.[2] Good advice, but the implications trouble me, since they suggest that staying healthy is largely in our hands and that falling victim to one of the many diseases of aging is a sign of personal irresponsibility, if not an actual moral lapse.

In *Illness as Metaphor,* Susan Sontag long ago noted that in our zeal to empower patients and enlist their will in fighting cancer, we developed myths and metaphors about the disease and those who suffered it that ultimately left patients feeling anxious about what they did to "cause" the cancer, and guilty about not being able to fight it successfully.[3] So it is now with aging, which, unlike cancer, is inevitable, but like it is unpredictable. Even when we follow all the advice—even when we never put another pat of butter on our bread, eat another morsel of red meat, or another bite of a trans-fat-filled cookie; even when we spend an hour at the gym and run five miles a day, do brain calisthenics in the morning and math equations in the evening—our bodies and brains seem to have a mind and a timetable of their own that remain outside our control. Yet the growing belief (myth?) that aging is a disease rather than a natural consequence of living has generated a steady stream of "good advice" about how we can beat back the clock, leaving us confused about what's possible and anxious about what we're doing "wrong" when we see evidence that we haven't succeeded.

But what about staying engaged? Surely that's something that *is* in our control—at least as long as we're healthy enough. Yes, but it's not so simple. People hardly need reminders to stay engaged with family, friends, even community. But what do you do when friends die and children live in distant places? And how do you stay involved in the community when you've outlived your welcome and no one is looking for your services—at least not those you want to offer?

Community organizations generally are happy to have older people volunteer to do routine work; it saves money and lightens the load of paid workers. But ask professional people who have tried to volunteer, and they'll tell you about the bureaucratic stumbling blocks that can make it difficult for them to give their services away.

In a public school system desperately in need of qualified teachers, the services of a retired college history professor I met were turned away because he wasn't properly credentialed by the state to teach high school. College, yes, but not high school.

A couple of years ago, I was invited to give the keynote lecture at the annual dinner of an organization that serves inner-city young people. In the course of my contacts with the group, several staff members told me that their training hadn't adequately prepared them to deal with some of the emotional problems they were seeing. *Good,* I thought; *here's something useful I can do.* I met with the director of the program and offered to develop and direct an in-service training program that would fill some of the gaps. He was delighted until he found out that his malpractice insurance wouldn't cover me as a volunteer, and without coverage, the organization couldn't take the risk. I would have been welcomed to answer the phones, clean up the place, organize the supplies, but they couldn't allow me to do what I do best and what they needed most.

But whatever difficulties the external roadblocks to engagement may present, the internal ones are at least as broad and deep. For one of the riddles of old age is how to manage the conflicting forces that emerge inside us: the pull toward disengagement that lies alongside the push toward engagement. The truth is: we want both. Not something that's easy to get in a society that thinks in opposites, that can't easily hold two thoughts in its head at the same time without assuming they contradict each other and that one has to go.

Not surprisingly, then, some older people, tired of listening to the exhortations to stay engaged from those who have little or no understanding of the complexity of our feelings at this time of life, are beginning to ask: What if we're tired of staying involved; what if, in the words of a retired newspaper columnist, "we want to be able to dodder"?[4] Well, maybe not dodder, but take our foot off the accelerator and proceed more slowly. "Does it occur to those prodding us toward the finish line that there's a subtle cruelty in asking us to 'stay in the fast lane' and 'go for it' at 70-something as we did at 30-something?" asks another seventy-something-year-old retiree.[5]

Not that anyone wants to argue for being inactive, maybe just to spend less time in pursuit of yet another goal, maybe just to have more time for *being* instead of *doing*.

Being! It's practically an un-American thought, especially in an era when we wear *doing* on our sleeve, when we tell each other about how busy we are in words that say complaint but in attitude that shouts pride. It's the latest status symbol, the public statement of our worth and importance. "Oh, I've been so busy, I just haven't had a chance to give you a call." "I wish we could do lunch, but I'm just too busy."

Leisure time? If by that we mean *being* leisurely, as in relaxed and unhurried, forget it. We're too busy *doing* leisure, too busy watching the clock and worrying about what's waiting for us when we're finished having "fun." Not a surprise, since nobody in this society gets points for taking it easy, for working less, for smelling the roses or enjoying the sun.

Americans today work 50 percent more than their West European counterparts, a shift from thirty years ago when people in those countries worked more.[6] French national law guarantees a 35-hour workweek, a minimum of five weeks paid vacation, plus eleven public holidays.[7] We average 42.7 hours a week,[8] generally have to be on the job three years or more before we can claim a two-week vacation, and have ten paid holidays annually—that is, if the company we work for honors all the national holidays, which isn't always the case. This, before we even begin to count up the after-hours work when we're "catching up" on e-mail, phone calls, paperwork, and all the other tasks we didn't get to during the day.

When, a few years ago, I decided to say goodbye to my last patient, my last student, my last lecture, I had no idea that the hardest part of the years ahead would be *not* being "too busy." After a lifetime of busy-ness and the rewards that came with it, I found myself bereft, lost in a sea of time with no idea how to live the days that stretched before me. Not that they didn't pass quickly. Ask anyone who's retired, and you'll hear about days that slide by, unheeded, unmarked, in some sense unlived. Perhaps even more than the money they need, it's this sense of uselessness, of time slipping by as if they're sleepwalking through it, that sends people back to work at jobs that are well below their skills and talents.

When I started this work, I thought I was writing a book about old age for those who are now living it, a book that would bring some corrective to the hyped-up media images about the glories of the "new old age," one that would validate their experience and affirm that their confused and contradictory feelings about this new stage of life are widely shared.

Now that I've finished, it seems also to be a cautionary tale for the children of the old, the baby boomers who will soon join the ranks of the over-sixty-fives and will confront the awesome and frightening reality that they still have another twenty or thirty years to live in a society that sees old age as repugnant at the same time that it expends precious resources on the dream of extending life still further. Paradoxical? Yes, but understandable if we see it in the context of the denial of death that pervades our culture. It's this deep-seated fear that underlies the end-of-life care that so often keeps people breathing even when they're not really living, and this that animates our quest to extend life still further while doing virtually nothing to ensure the quality of those added years.

For those boomers who may be reading these words, then, I have a message. Old age lasts a long time, and it will last even longer by the time you get here. But unlike your parents who stumbled into these years without a clue, you have a choice about how you'll live them. You can go on believing all the cheery good news about the new old age, that sixty is the new forty and eighty the new sixty, that if you eat right, sleep right, exercise your body and your brain right, you'll never get *really* old. Or you can take a long, hard look at the realities of the social and personal world of aging I've described here.

Right now, you're living in a country that's as unprepared for your old age as you are, a country where economists and policy analysts worry that you're "the monster at our door," the "elephant in the room"[9] that threatens to bring the nation to its economic knees, the one that will break the Social Security bank and drain Medicare with your health needs, which grow exponentially with each decade of life.

Whatever the merit of these worst-fear scenarios, one thing is certain: in the next two decades 78 million of you will enter the ranks of the aged. *That's 26 percent of the current population.* Without major changes in social priorities, public policy, and a culture with a long history of deeply ingrained prejudice against the old, you'll find yourself coping with the social and personal vicissitudes of getting old in America without much help from any quarter.

You can choose to walk blithely into that future believing that none of this means you, or you can say, as you did once before about a war you refused to fight: "Hell no!" Only this time, you have no choice but to go. For while you may be able to stave off some of the worst effects of aging for a while, I promise that all of you—sooner perhaps for some, later for others—*will* grow old in a society that abhors old age and whose social institutions reflect its cultural attitudes.

Once, long ago, you coined the slogan "The personal is political." It was the banner under which you transformed the cultural face of America, the flag you carried as you stopped a war, changed the sexual norms of the nation, ignited a feminist revolution that transformed both public and private life, and converted the perception of homosexuality from perversion to just another sexual orientation. Your voices have been subdued in the last couple of decades, quieted by the pressures of your daily lives —working, raising the children, staying ahead of the bills. It would be nice to take a rest as you move into the next stage of your life; you've earned it. But not yet.

Robert Butler, the former director of the National Institute of Aging and arguably the foremost scholar and advocate for the aged in America, spoke recently about the prospects for your future: "I think they're in for a hell of a time, because society is not prepared for them. And I don't think they're a bit prepared for old age. . . . If they're able to [make any changes] it will mostly benefit Generations X and Y. The baby boomers are, quite frankly, a generation at risk."[10]

As he speaks today, he's right. But it doesn't have to be that way. Your numbers alone, if you can organize them to collective action, give you the power to seriously dent, if not fully change, the cultural assumptions and social policy that now dominate aging in twenty-first-century America.

Acknowledgments

In the background of every book stands a small army of unseen contributors. Foremost among them in this case are the people who participated in this research. No words can repay their generosity in welcoming me into their homes, their thoughts, and their feelings. I can only hope they'll agree that what I've written here not only reproduces their words but is true to the spirit in which they spoke them.

My thanks also to the friends and colleagues who read various parts of the work in progress and shared their thoughts with me: Joan Cole, Laura Dawson, Sandra Shane DuBow, Peter Finkelstein, Jackie Hackel, Anne and Ernie Lieberman, and Terry Stein.

I owe a special vote of gratitude to two friends—Diane Ehrensaft and Michael Kimmel—who have, for more years than any of us cares to count, been among my nearest and dearest. They have always been there for me both personally and professionally, and this was no exception. They listened patiently to my thoughts, read what I wrote, supported me when I was right, argued with me when I was not, and in the process made this a better, stronger book than it would have been without their wise counsel.

Then there are those who have been so close to the work from beginning to end that they are more foreground than background. Their contributions to my life are too numerous to mention, so it's easier to talk about how much they affected this book. They joined me in more discussions about aging than I can count, read every word of every draft, responded with the kind of critical acuity every writer dreams about, and not least, were the cheering section that kept me going when the "going" got tough. For their generosity of both intellect and heart in these behind-the-scenes roles, I am deeply grateful to Barbara Artson, for more than three decades, the sister I always wished for; Dorothy Jones, my oldest friend, the one who "knew me when"; and Alix Shulman, more recently in my life, but no less steadfast in her involvement with this work.

As always, my editor, Helene Atwan, has been a wise and gentle guide from the first day to the last. It was her phone call that started me on the journey that led to writing this book—a conversation for which I'll always be grateful. Since then, her good humor along with her steady support, encouragement, and friendship have enriched both this book and my life.

Thanks, also, to Allison Trzop and Lisa Sacks for making me laugh. And a grateful nod as well to all the other women and men at Beacon Press who shepherded this book through the production process and brought it into the world.

Finally, no words of love and gratitude can fully express what I owe to my daughter, Marci Rubin, and my husband, Hank Rubin. Marci, who is all a mother could wish for, was with me every step of the way in this project, bringing to it both her keen intellect and her unwavering emotional support. Her comments, her criticisms, and our many discussions left an unmistakable imprint on the final product. Hank, always there, always encouraging, always offering loving support, has been my partner, my lover, and my mainstay for the forty-five best years of my life. To them I dedicate this book.

Notes

Chapter One: Through the Looking Glass

1. Betty Friedan, *The Fountain of Age* (New York: Simon & Schuster, 1993).

2. Charlie Hauck, "My Plan to Save Network Television," *New York Times*, September 16, 2006.

3. Simone de Beauvoir, *The Coming of Age*, translated by Patrick O'Brian (New York: Putnam, 1972), 5.

4. Lillian B. Rubin, *Tangled Lives: Daughters, Mothers, and the Crucible of Aging* (Boston: Beacon Press, 2000).

5. In preparation for writing this book, I conducted fifty-two face-to-face interviews with women and men between the ages of sixty-five and ninety-two, and also talked with adult children—sometimes the children of the people I interviewed, often not. Equally important to the shape and content of the work are the dozens of informal over-the-table conversations I've been having for the last several years with acquaintances, friends, and colleagues, and not least, my personal experience and understanding of what it means to grow old.

6. Gina Kolata, "So Big and Healthy Grandpa Wouldn't Even Know You," *New York Times*, July 30, 2006.

7. U.S. Census Bureau, Census 2000 PHC-T-13, "Population and Ranking Tables of the Older Population for the United States, Puerto Rico."

8. Ibid.

Chapter Two: Out of the Closet

1. Ken Dychtwald, *Age Power: How the 21st Century Will Be Ruled by the New Old* (New York: Jeremy P. Tarcher/Putnam, 2000); Ken Dychtwald and Daniel J. Kadlec, *The Power Years: A User's Guide to the Rest of Your Life* (Hoboken, N.J.: Wiley, 2005).

2. James Barron and Anemona Hartocollis, "As Mrs. Astor Slips, the Grandson Blames the Son," *New York Times*, July 27, 2006.

3. M. S. Lachs and K. Pillemer, "Elder Abuse," *Lancet* 364, no. 9441 (October 2–8, 2004), 1263–72.

4. Richard Posner, *Aging and Old Age* (Chicago: University of Chicago Press, 1995), 202–3.

5. U.S. Census Bureau, "Older Americans Month Celebrated in May," Facts for Features CB05-FF/07–2, April 25, 2005.

6. Anti-aging has become such big business that, in just a few years, the academy's membership has grown from a few hundred physicians and scientists to the seventeen thousand they now claim. And they are not alone. Dr. Allen Mintz, chief medical officer and CEO of the Cenegenics Medical Institute, claims to have developed a protocol that guarantees a new kind of aging. For $1,000 a month or more, doctors associated with the institute provide treatment that includes the injection of performance-enhancing drugs, some of them illegal except under clearly specified conditions, like testosterone, human growth hormone, and dehydroepiandrosterone (DHEA)—all substances that can get athletes banned from their sports.

7. Stanley Tucci's character in the 2006 film *The Devil Wears Prada* strips away the young assistant's pride in her size six with an acid-tongued reminder that "six is the new fourteen." Vanity sizing of women's clothes isn't just a throwaway line in a film. While American women are getting heavier—on average weighing about 155 pounds at five feet four inches—sizes continue to dip, so much so that Banana Republic now offers size 00 (probably formerly size 2 or 4), and other designers have introduced a size called "sub-zero."

8. Pam Belluck, "As Minds Age, What's Next? Brain Calisthenics," *New York Times*, December 27, 2006.

9. Kate Scannell, "An Aging Un-American," *New England Journal of Medicine* 355, no. 14 (October 5, 2006), 1415–17.

Chapter Three: Staying Younger While Getting Older

1. Michael B. Katz, *The Irony of Early School Reform: Educational Innovation in Mid-Nineteenth Century Massachusetts* (Cambridge, Mass.: Harvard University Press, 1968).

2. Diane Ehrensaft, *Spoiling Childhood: How Well-Meaning Parents Are Giving Children Too Much — But Not What They Need* (New York: Guilford Press, 1999).

3. Janny Scott, "Out of College, but Now Living in Urban Dorms," *New York Times*, July 13, 2006, paints a compelling picture of young people who can't fully grow up because they can't earn enough money to find an apartment, let alone to get married and have children.

4. Lillian B. Rubin, *Women of a Certain Age: The Midlife Search for Self* (New York: Harper & Row, 1979).

5. Rand Richards Cooper, "Fatherhood, I Now Learn, Is a Young Man's Game," *New York Times*, August 20, 2006.

Chapter Four: Does Age Count Anymore?

1. Paul B. Baltes and Jacqui Smith, "New Frontiers in the Future of Aging: From Successful Aging of the Young Old to the Dilemmas of the Fourth Age," *Gerontology* 49, no. 2 (2003), 123–35.

2. Philip Roth, *Everyman* (Boston: Houghton Mifflin, 2006), 103.

3. Cited in Simone de Beauvoir, *The Coming of Age*, translated by Patrick O'Brian (New York: Putnam, 1972), 5.

4. D. L. Ashliman, ed. and trans., *Aging and Death in Folklore* (Pittsburgh: University of Pittsburgh, 1997–2005), www.pitt.edu/~dash/aging .html.

5. James Hastings, ed., *Encyclopaedia of Religion and Ethics*, vol. 1 (New York: Chase, Scribner & Sons, 1910), 5.

6. Sophocles, *Oedipus at Colonus*, in Hastings, ed., *Encyclopaedia of Religion and Ethics*, 469.

7. *The Pastor of Hermas*, in Alexander Roberts and James Donaldson, eds., *The Anti-Nicene Fathers*, vol. 2 (Grand Rapids, Mich.: Eerdmans, 1962).

8. Saint Augustine, Sermon 108, in *A Select Library of Nicene and Post-Nicene Fathers of the Christian Church*, edited by Philip Schaff (Grand Rapids, Mich.: Eerdmans, 1956), 440.

9. Michel de Montaigne, *The Complete Essays*, translated by M. A. Screech (New York: Penguin Classics, 1993).

10. Betty Friedan, *The Fountain of Age* (New York: Simon & Schuster, 1993), 36.

Chapter Five: The Marriage of Self and Society

1. So concerned are these communities to protect their homogeneity that they often have rules limiting the amount of time grandchildren may visit.

2. Nora Ephron, *I Feel Bad about My Neck, and Other Thoughts on Being a Woman* (New York: Knopf, 2006), 129; 5.

Chapter Six: The Golden Years? They've Gotta Be Kidding!

1. Lillian B. Rubin, *Women of a Certain Age: The Midlife Search for Self* (New York: Harper & Row, 1979), 123.

2. U.S. Census Bureau, Table 101, "Age-Adjusted Death Rates by Race and Sex, 1920–2002," *Statistical Abstract of the United States* (Washington, D.C.: U.S. Government Printing Office, 2006).

3. Jacques Steinberg, "Mike Wallace Says He Will Retire from '60 Minutes' in Spring," *New York Times*, March 15, 2006.

4. Lillian B. Rubin, *Worlds of Pain: Life in the Working-Class Family* (New York: Basic Books, 1976) and *Families on the Fault Line: America's Working Class Speaks about the Family, the Economy, Race, and Ethnicity* (New York: HarperCollins, 1994). There is a large body of evidence showing the relationship between male unemployment and greatly increased

rates of depression, alcoholism, and domestic violence—evidence that supports the proposition that work, whatever it is, is central to a man's ability to maintain his identity and self-respect.

5. Matthew Greenwald & Associates, "2006 Retirement Confidence Survey," in U.S. Bureau of Labor Statistics, *Employment and Earnings* (Washington, D.C.: Congressional Budget Office, January 2006). Median net worth of all Americans was $55,000 in 2000, with home equity constituting the largest share. U.S. Census Bureau, "Net Worth and Asset Ownership: 1998 and 2000," *Current Population Reports*.

6. Patrick Purcell, *Retirement Savings and Household Wealth: Trends from 2001–2004* (New York: Institute for Workplace Studies, Cornell University, 2006).

7. In a table comparing rates of savings in American households, the U.S. Bureau of Labor Statistics reports that savings dropped from 7 percent in 1990 to 1.2 percent in 2004. Table 659, "Personal Income and Its Disposition, 1990–2004," *Statistical Abstract of the United States* (Washington, D.C.: U.S. Government Printing Office, 2006).

8. About one-quarter of families at the bottom two-fifths of the income scale carry a debt load of 40 percent. Steven Greenhouse, "Borrowers We Be," *New York Times*, September 3, 2006.

9. Jack Rosenthal, "The Age Boom," *New York Times Magazine*, March 9, 1977.

10. Mary Cantwell, "Still At Work on a Self," *New York Times Magazine*, March 9, 1997.

11. Women over sixty-five are three times more likely to be widowed than their male counterparts. Among men in this age group, 71 percent are married and living with their spouses and only 14 percent are widowed. U.S. Census Bureau, "Older Americans Month Celebrated in May," Facts for Features CB05-FF/07–2, April 25, 2005.

12. www.timegoesby.net.

13. See Robert N. Butler, *Why Survive? Being Old in America* (New York: HarperCollins, 1985).

14. Quoted in Claudia Dreifus, "Focusing on the Issue of Aging, and Growing Into the Job," *New York Times*, November 14, 2006.

15. Frank Bruni, "Be Merry, Not Ancient," *New York Times*, April 9, 2006.

Chapter Seven: . . . And Now About Sex

1. Philip Roth's 2006 novel *Everyman*, exploring the dark side of aging, is a refreshing exception. The protagonist rages about his body's betrayal, not least of which is the impairment of his sexual functioning.

2. Gail Sheehy, *Sex and the Seasoned Woman: Pursuing the Passionate Life* (New York: Random House, 2007).

3. Abraham Morgentaler, *The Viagra Myth: The Surprising Impact on Love and Relationships* (San Francisco: Jossey-Bass, 2003).

4. Jessie Bernard, *The Future of Marriage* (New York: Bantam Books, 1973).

5. Edmund Leites, *The Puritan Conscience and Modern Sexuality* (New Haven, Conn.: Yale University Press, 1986).

6. Sigmund Freud, *Three Essays on Sexuality* (New York: Avon Books, 1962).

7. Not surprising, perhaps, since they were all women whose sexual behavior—even their sexual desires—were formed in the pre–sexual revolution era, when boys were warned they'd grow hair on their palms and damage their brains if they masturbated, and no one even talked about girls and masturbation, since it was assumed they didn't have any spontaneous sexual desires.

8. A British study with a sample of 179 men and women sixty years and over asked questions about specific sexual behaviors—mutual stroking, masturbation, or intercourse—and found that 82 percent said no to any such activity in the year before they were questioned. Of that 82 percent, 63 percent were women. Terri Beth Greenberg, Sherry C. Pomerantz, and Veronika Karmer-Feeling, "Sexuality in Older Adults: Behaviours and Preferences," *Age and Ageing* 34 (2005), 475–80.

Chapter Eight: The Shrinking Ties That Bind

1. Lynn Smith-Lovin, Miller McPherson, and Matthew Brashears, "Social Isolation in America," *American Sociological Review* 71, no. 3 (June 2006), 353–75.

2. See Lillian B. Rubin, *Just Friends: The Role of Friendship in Our Lives* (New York: Harper & Row, 1985), chapter 4, "Men, Women and Friends: The Differences Between Us," 59–79.

3. Doris Grumbach, "What Old Age Is *Really* Like," *New York Times,* November 1, 1998.

4. Doris Grumbach, *Extra Innings: A Memoir* (New York: Norton, 1993).

Chapter Nine: Hey Folks, You're Spending My Inheritance

1. John J. Havens and Paul G. Schervish, *Millionaires and the Millennium: New Estimates of the Forthcoming Wealth Transfer and the Prospects for a Golden Age of Philanthropy* (Boston: Boston College Social Welfare Research Institute, 1999).

2. A recent feature story on the American Banking Association's Web site, www.banking.com/ABA/, "Questions about the 'Inheritance Boom,'" by Denise Duclaux, suggests the far smaller number of $10.4 trillion.

3. John J. Havens and Paul G. Schervish, *Why the $41 Trillion Wealth Transfer Estimate Is Still Valid: A Review of Challenges and Questions* (Boston: Boston College Social Welfare Research Institute, 2003).

4. According to the U.S. Census Bureau, 81 percent of householders sixty-five and over own their own homes. "Older Americans Month Celebrated in May," Facts for Features CB05-FF/07-2, April 25, 2005.

5. Bob Morris, "Stop Spending My Inheritance," *New York Times,* July 30, 2006.

6. See Roberta Satow, *Doing the Right Thing: Taking Care of Your Elderly Parents Even If They Didn't Take Care of You* (New York: Jeremy P. Tarcher, 2005), for a compassionate and forgiving exploration of caregivers' conflicts when relationships have been strained by conflict.

7. The CEO Network, www.theceonetwork.com/facts/html, August 24, 2006.

8. U.S. Census Bureau, "Money Income of Families by Race and Hispanic Origin," *Statistical Abstract of the United States* (Washington: D.C.: U.S. Government Printing Office, 2006).

9. Statistics on the over-sixty-fives are from U.S. Census Bureau, "Older Americans Month Celebrated in May," Facts for Features CB05-FF.07–2, April 25, 2005.

10. Ibid.

Chapter Ten: Taking Care of Mom and Dad

1. Cathy Booth, "Taking Care of Our Aging Parents," *Time*, August 30, 1999.

2. James Atlas, "The Sandwich Generation," *New Yorker*, October 13, 1997, 54–60.

3. U.S. Department of Health and Human Services, National Center for Health Statistics, "Limitation of Activity: All Ages: U.S. 2000–2004."

4. It may be, as some predict, that this is the inevitable consequence of an industrialized society and that, as the Chinese economy continues to expand, the culture of familism will crumble. My own view is that while it may fray, it will not collapse entirely, at least not any time in the foreseeable future. We need only look at third- and fourth-generation Chinese Americans here in the United States to see the staying power of these old cultural norms, as even well-assimilated families continue to expect a far greater level of responsibility and obligation than do most American families.

5. Jane Gross, "Forensic Skills Seek to Uncover Elder Abuse," *New York Times*, September 27, 2006.

6. Eileen Alt Powell, "Study: Communities Unready for the Elderly," *New York Times*, September 27, 2006.

7. H.R. 4993, Elder Justice Act of 2006.

8. U.S. Census Bureau, "Geographic Mobility: 2002–2003," *Current Population Reports* (March 2004).

Chapter Eleven: Oh My God, We're Old!

1. Kate Scannell, "An Aging Un-American," *New England Journal of Medicine* 355, no. 14 (October 5, 2006), 1415–17.

2. I'm aware that's soon to be sixty-seven, but for my generation, sixty-five was the magic number.

3. Alzheimer's Foundation of America, "Statistics," www.alzfdn.org/alzheimers/statistics/shtml.

4. In California alone, 100,000 reports of abuse were filed in 2003, accounting for 20 percent of the 500,000 reports nationwide. But there is widespread agreement among professionals dealing with the old that these numbers underrepresent the problem. See Jane Gross, "Forensic Skills Seek to Uncover Elder Abuse," *New York Times*, September 27, 2006.

Chapter Twelve: It's Better Than the Alternative, Isn't It?

1. Sherwin B. Nuland, *How We Die: Reflections on Life's Final Chapter* (New York: Knopf, 1994), 255.

2. Susan Sontag, *Illness as Metaphor* (New York: Farrar, Straus and Giroux, 1978), 55–56.

3. David Rieff, "Illness as More Than Metaphor," *New York Times Magazine*, December 4, 2005.

4. See Karen E. Steinhauser et al., "In Search of a Good Death: Observations of Patients, Families, and Providers," *Annals of Internal Medicine* 132, no. 10 (May 2000), 825–32.

5. State of Oregon, Department of Human Services, *Eighth Annual Report on Oregon's Death with Dignity Act*, March 9, 2006.

6. Jan Hoffman, "The Last Word on the Last Breath," *New York Times*, October 10, 2006.

7. Nuland, *How We Die*, 255.

8. Quoted in Hoffman, "The Last Word on the Last Breath."

9. Ernest Becker, *The Denial of Death* (New York: Free Press, 1973), 15.

10. Cited by Ronald Blythe in his introduction to Leo Tolstoy, *The Death of Ivan Ilyich* (New York: Bantam Books, 1981), 10.

11. Becker, *The Denial of Death*, xii.

12. Nuland, *How We Die*, 268.

Chapter Thirteen: One Last Word

1. Henry Amiel, 1874, quoted in George E. Vaillant, *Aging Well* (Boston: Little, Brown, 2002).

2. See, for example, John W. Rowe and Robert L. Kahn, *Successful Aging* (New York: Pantheon, 1998), a book based on a national study funded by the MacArthur Foundation, in which the authors define the three components of successful aging: avoid disease, stay physically and mentally healthy, and engage with life.

3. Susan Sontag, *Illness as Metaphor* (New York: Farrar, Straus, and Giroux, 1978).

4. Henry Fountain, "Old and Overscheduled: No, You Can't Just Dodder," *New York Times*, May 15, 2005.

5. Melvin Maddocks, "Long Live Decrepitude," *New York Times*, August 27, 1999.

6. Edward C. Prescott and W. P. Carey, "Why Do Americans Work So Much More Than Europeans?" *Federal Reserve Bank of Minneapolis Quarterly Review* 28, no. 1 (July 2004), 2–13.

7. Gordon T. Anderson, "Should America Be France? Do Americans Work Too Much?" *CNN/Money*, October 9, 2003.

8. United States Department of Labor, Bureau of Labor Statistics, Current Population Survey, Table A-26, "Persons in Non-Agricultural Industries by Class of Workers and Usual Full- or Part-Time Status." Table A-27, which analyzes these data by gender, shows that men, on the average, work 44.1 hours a week, women 41. The difference when marital status is separated out is minimal: 44.6 for men, 40.9 for women.

9. Robert J. Samuelson, "The Monster at Our Door," *Newsweek*, September 10, 2006; Robin Toner and David E. Rosenbaum, "Age: The Elephant in the Room," *New York Times*, June 12, 2006.

10. Quoted in Claudia Dreifus, "Focusing on the Issue of Aging, and Growing Into the Job," *New York Times*, November 14, 2006.